QUALITY DIMENSIONS OF A SCHOOL

DR DHEERAJ MEHROTRA

Contents

Preface

*Achieving excellence in education transcends being a mere benchmark; it constitutes an ongoing process. We, as constituents, educators, and administrators, endeavour to establish settings that nurture comprehensive growth, rigorous academic inquiry, and a climate of ongoing enhancement. The book **"Quality Dimensions of a School"** examines the various complex elements contributing to defining and forming a school's quality.*

By capitalizing on extensive research, years of experience, and the perspectives of educational authorities worldwide, this book provides a thorough examination of the multifaceted elements that comprise a school's quality. This comprehensive analysis encompasses every aspect, including infrastructure, leadership, community engagement, curriculum design, and teaching methodologies. It offers practical strategies, case studies, and reflections to assist educational institutions in achieving excellence.

This book facilitates an exploration of self-discovery, introspection, and metamorphosis. May it furnish educators and school administrators with a navigational guide through the intricacies of quality education, guaranteeing that each child is exposed to the most exceptional learning experience.

Dr Dheeraj Mehrotra

Author

CHAPTER ONE

Defining Quality in Education

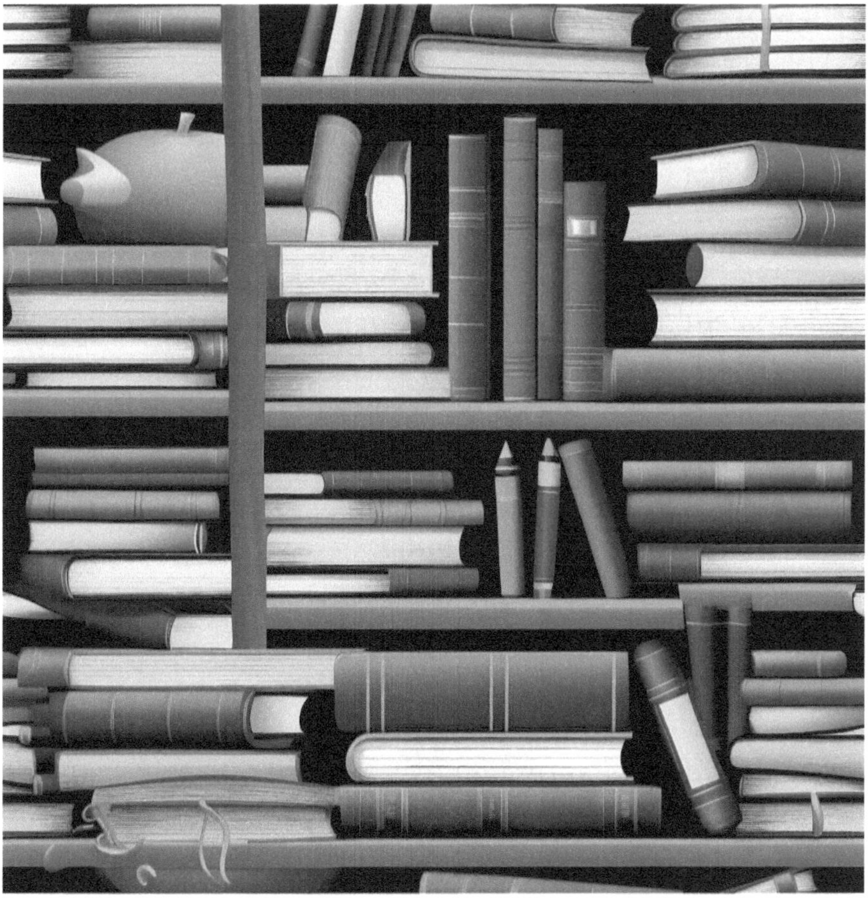

Acquiring an Understanding of Educational Quality:

A high-quality education considers all the factors that make lessons interesting and informative for students. It encompasses more than just academic performance; it also considers things like students' involvement, teachers' efficacy, and the learning environment as a whole. A high-quality education should give students the character traits, practical abilities, and theoretical understanding to thrive in a dynamic and unpredictable global economy.

Elements crucial to educational excellence comprise:

Curriculum and learning experiences should be meaningful to students in relation to their lives, future goals, and society's demands.

There should be no barriers to a high-quality education for each student, regardless of their family's financial situation, race, gender, or physical or mental abilities.

Students should be enthusiastic participants in their education, encouraging one another to think critically, creatively, and with an open mind.

Assessment:

To help students improve and succeed, assessment methods should be trustworthy, valid, and fair.

Quality instructors are essential for providing students with effective education, developing strong relationships with them, and creating a supportive learning environment.

Schools should provide safe, welcoming, and supportive learning environments that encourage students to work together, respect one another, and care for themselves.

Partnerships in the Community:

When schools, families, and other community members work together, they may give students more tools, support, and opportunities to succeed in school.

Critical Role of Quality Dimension Definitions:

There are some reasons why it is crucial to define education quality dimensions:

Clarity:

When quality dimensions are specified precisely, educators, legislators, and stakeholders can agree on what constitutes a high-quality education.

Evaluation:

Educational programs, policies, and practices can be assessed based on quality factors.

Upgrading:

By focusing on particular quality dimensions, educational institutions and schools can pinpoint problem areas and apply evidence-based solutions to raise the quality bar across the board.

Accountability is a key component of quality dimensions, and it ensures that all of the school's money and time go toward the right things.

Defining quality dimensions helps promote equity in education. These dimensions pinpoint inequalities and direct efforts to rectify them.

Views on Quality Education from the Past:

Throughout history, society's values, cultural norms, and educational philosophies have moulded different viewpoints on quality education. A few viewpoints from the past regarding high-quality education are:

Classical Education:

The ancient Greeks and Romans valued the study of literature, philosophy, and the arts as a means of cultivating good citizenship, intelligence, and character.

Standardization, discipline, obedience, and acquiring fundamental reading, writing, and arithmetic abilities were hallmarks of the Industrial Revolution-era curriculum, which sought to prepare pupils for life in the workforce better.

Educators like John Dewey, who belonged to the progressive school of thought in the early 20th century, pushed for a shift in focus from teachers to students, emphasising hands-on experience, analytical thinking, and overall growth and development.

Issues including access, equity, curriculum reform, teacher training, and assessment procedures have been at the centre of numerous educational reform movements that have sprung up in the twentieth and twenty-first centuries, all intending to raise the bar for student learning.

One way to better understand how education has developed and how various viewpoints have impacted current methods is to look back at how different eras have defined quality education. These viewpoints still shape efforts to define and promote educational quality.

Aside from the significance of identifying quality dimensions and looking at quality education from a historical perspective, here are some other things to think about when trying to grasp the idea of quality in education:

Acquiring an Understanding of Educational Quality:

Access to high-quality education is more important than ever in our globally linked world to remain competitive in today's global economy. A nation's ability to adjust to new technologies, economic conditions, and social norms is directly correlated to the quality of its educational system.

The ability to keep learning and growing is a hallmark of a quality education system, which encourages students to pursue further education throughout their lives.

Quality education fosters active and informed citizenship, equipping individuals to engage actively in democratic communities and make beneficial social changes.

Integrity, empathy, respect, and social responsibility are just a few of the ethical qualities that a good education imparts. They help students develop into responsible and caring adults who contribute to society in positive ways.

Quality education promotes awareness, appreciation, and knowledge of other cultures, viewpoints, and global challenges, which in turn encourages global citizenship in an increasingly interdependent world.

Critical Role of Quality Dimension Definitions:

Improving Over Time: By outlining quality criteria, we may evaluate current conditions, pinpoint problem areas, and devise specific solutions, all of which contribute to ongoing progress.

Allocating Resources: Well-defined quality dimensions allow for more informed judgments when allocating resources, which in turn helps to maximize the impact of limited funds on improving educational quality.

Involving Stakeholders: Including stakeholders while developing quality dimensions increases support, cooperation, and ownership of quality improvement projects.

Policies and standards based on quality are developed at the local, national, and worldwide levels to promote equity, excellence, and accountability in education.

Research and Evaluation: Researchers can measure the success of educational interventions, programs, and policies using defined quality dimensions as a basis for their research and evaluation studies.

Views on Quality Education from the Past:

Social Mobility:

Throughout history, individuals have overcome socioeconomic barriers and attained upward mobility by gaining access to high-quality educational opportunities.

Cultural transmission involves the passing down of cultural artifacts, practices, beliefs, and information from one generation to the next.

Education Democratization:

Efforts to promote social justice, equality, and inclusion in education have, throughout time, increased the number of underprivileged and marginalized students with access to high-quality education.

Technological progress has expanded access to high-quality educational resources and opportunities and facilitated new approaches to instruction and evaluation.

Given the interrelated nature of excellent education in this age of globalization and the impact of global trends, policies, and movements, international collaboration and cooperation are crucial for enhancing educational quality.

Taking into account these other viewpoints can help us better understand quality education, its importance, and its historical development. This broader viewpoint guides us in our pursuit to identify, promote, and improve educational quality in various contexts and situations.

Acquiring an Understanding of Educational Quality:

Quality education emphasizes student-centred approaches, prioritising learners' unique abilities, interests, and needs. Every learner is different and needs individualized attention to reach his or her maximum potential; our method considers that.

Effective work in various cultural settings and understanding and addressing global issues are essential competencies in today's interdependent world. A well-rounded education can help students develop these competencies.

Skills for Life:

A good education goes beyond imparting facts and figures; it also teaches students to think critically, communicate effectively, work together, be creative, and overcome obstacles. These abilities depend on the ability to do well in school and in the real world.

Emotional Intelligence, Self-Awareness, Empathy, and Social Competence: High-quality education prioritizes socio-emotional learning. These skills are crucial for forming healthy relationships, controlling one's emotions, and making sound judgments.

Critical Role of Quality Dimension Definitions:

Schools and other educational institutions can establish goals, monitor progress, and make data-driven decisions based on the defined quality characteristics to improve educational results over time.

Policymakers and education leaders can strategically deploy resources by identifying certain quality aspects. This way, investments will align with priorities and have the greatest impact on student learning and well-being.

Educators, students, families, and communities all have a stake in bettering educational outcomes, and defining quality dimensions promotes stakeholder participation and cooperation.

Views on Quality Education from the Past:

Various communities' values, beliefs, and priorities are reflected in the diverse historical views on quality education, which are influenced by cultural and contextual factors. Traditional indigenous education systems frequently prioritise holistic development, communal values, and environmental care.

The philosophical underpinnings of education: Various schools of thought, including idealism, realism, pragmatism, and existentialism, have shaped educational aims, practices, and results across time and space.

Renaissance, Enlightenment, and Romanticism are just a few educational revolutions that have shaped our understanding of what it means to have a good education by emphasizing humanism, rationalism, individualism, and creativity.

By delving into these supplementary topics, we enhance our comprehension of quality education, its components, and its historical development; this, in turn, paves the way for well-informed debates and efforts to raise the bar for all students' educational experiences.

CHAPTER TWO

Pedagogy and Curriculum

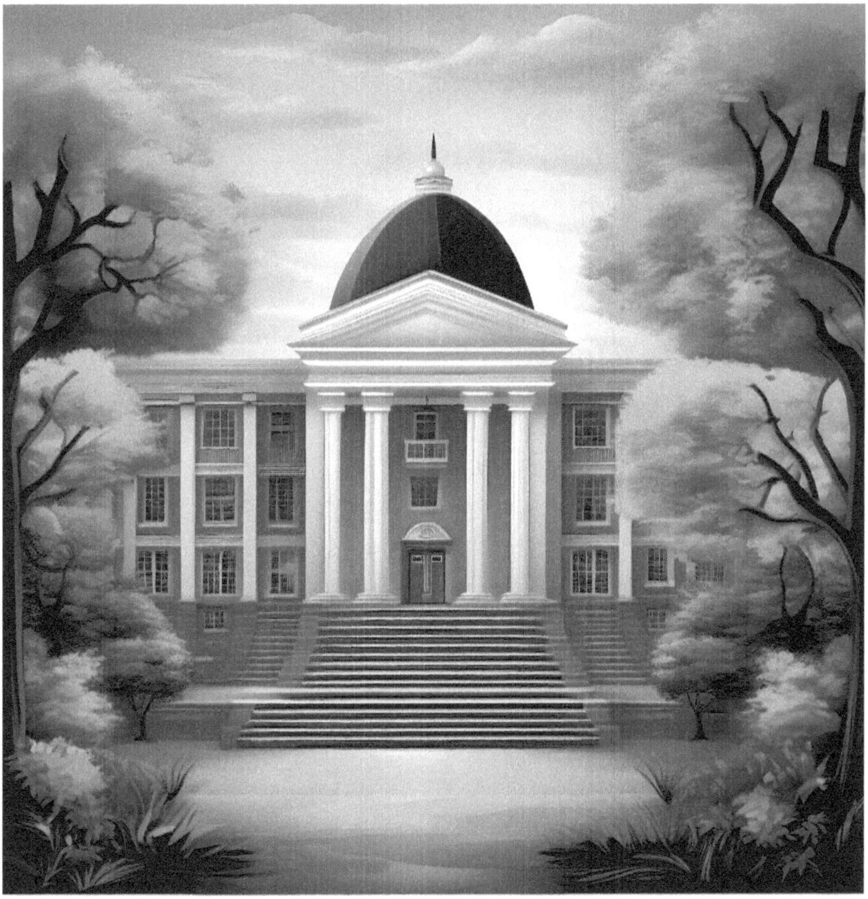

Developing a comprehensive curriculum structure involves several key steps, especially when integrating novel pedagogical methodologies and emphasizing differentiation and personalization in instruction and learning.

Here's a structured approach:

Needs Assessment and Goal Setting:

Conduct a thorough needs assessment to understand the learners' needs, interests, and abilities.

Set clear educational goals and objectives that align with educational standards and outcomes.

Curriculum Design Framework:

Choose a curriculum design model that suits your educational context, such as the Tyler, Taba, or Wiggins and McTighe's Understanding by Design (UbD) framework.

Adapt the chosen framework to incorporate novel pedagogical methodologies, such as project-based learning, inquiry-based learning, flipped classroom, or blended learning.

Content Selection and Sequencing:

Select relevant and engaging content that aligns with the curriculum goals and objectives.

Sequence the content logically to scaffold learning and ensure progressive skill development.

Pedagogical Approaches:

Integrate novel pedagogical methodologies to enhance engagement and promote deeper learning.

Consider strategies such as active, collaborative, problem-based, and experiential learning.

Incorporate technology appropriately to support instruction and facilitate personalized learning experiences.

Assessment and Evaluation:

Design authentic and varied assessment methods to assess students' understanding, skills, and competencies.

Implement formative assessments to provide ongoing feedback and guide instruction.

Use summative assessments to evaluate students' overall achievement of learning objectives.

Differentiation and Personalization:

Implement strategies for differentiation to accommodate diverse learning needs and preferences.

Provide opportunities for student choice and autonomy in learning paths and activities.

Offer personalized learning experiences through adaptive learning technologies, individualized projects, or customized learning pathways.

Continuous Improvement:

Review and revise the curriculum based on student, educator, and stakeholder feedback.

Stay updated on emerging research, best practices, and educational trends to inform curriculum design decisions.

Encourage a culture of reflection and professional development among educators to continually enhance teaching practices and curriculum effectiveness.

Following this comprehensive approach, you can develop a curriculum structure that integrates novel pedagogical methodologies while prioritizing differentiation and personalization in instruction and learning.

CHAPTER THREE

Infrastructure and Resources

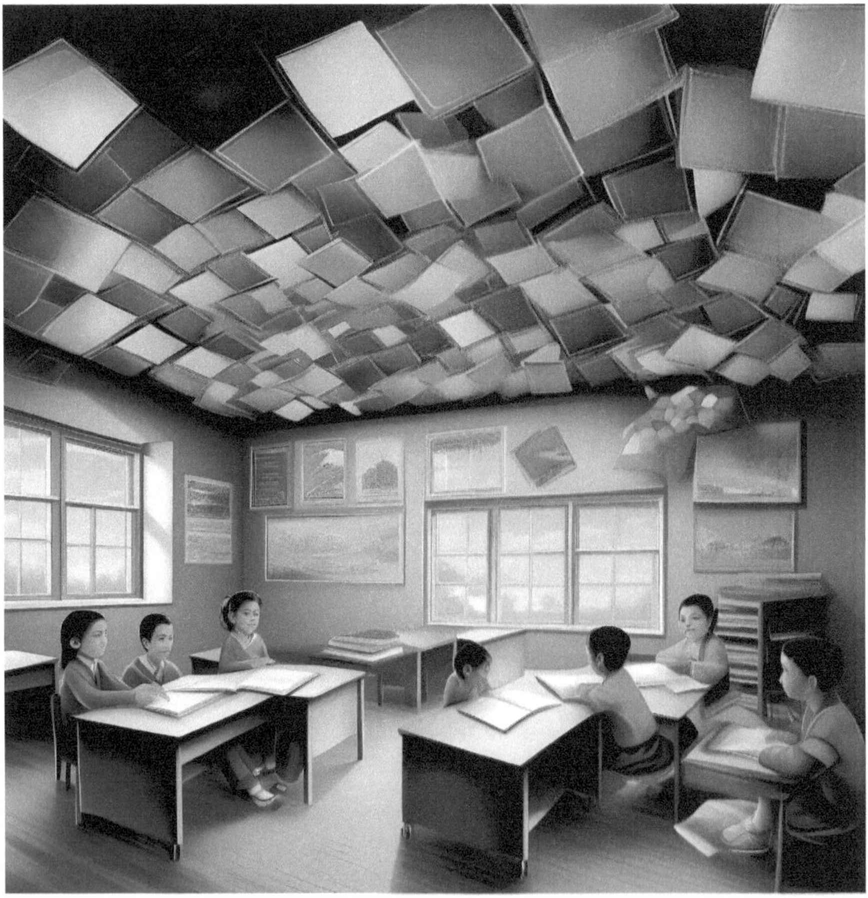

Establishing optimal learning environments

Creating ideal learning settings is essential for cultivating student engagement, facilitating academic achievement, and fostering comprehensive growth. An ideal learning environment includes physical, social, emotional, and cognitive elements that establish a supportive and favourable setting for learning. This post will examine the essential elements and tactics for creating ideal learning environments in educational contexts.

The physical environment substantially impacts the formation of the learning experience. An intelligently planned classroom arrangement featuring generous space, abundant natural light, comfortable seating, and suitable materials cultivates a feeling of security and inclusion. Arranging educational resources, such as books, instructional materials, and technology, in a convenient and orderly fashion fosters self-reliance and enhances learning. Incorporating natural features like plants or outdoor learning spaces can promote well-being and foster creativity.

Social Environment: Creating a favourable and all-encompassing social environment promotes cooperation, interaction, and shared admiration among students and educators. A supportive and respectful classroom culture can be achieved by establishing classroom standards and expectations that encourage compassion, empathy, and active listening. Promoting peer connection, engaging in group activities, and fostering cooperative learning enhances social-emotional development and cultivates interpersonal skills. Efficient classroom management tactics, such as explicit communication, uniform behaviour reinforcement, and conflict resolution procedures, aid in upholding a favourable social atmosphere and reducing disturbances.

Emotional Environment: Establishing an emotionally secure and supportive setting is essential for fostering pupils' well-being, adaptability, and favourable psychological state. Teachers may cultivate emotional intelligence and self-awareness in students by recognizing and affirming their emotions, offering outlets for self-expression, and instructing them in techniques for handling stress and anxiety. Students' growth mindset can be nurtured by providing praise, encouragement, and constructive feedback. This approach enables students to willingly take on challenges, gain insights from their failures, and persist in overcoming hurdles. Moreover, fostering a feeling of membership and embracing diversity through inclusive methodologies and culturally sensitive instruction creates confidence and enhances connections within the educational community.

The cognitive environment combines instructional tactics, curriculum design, and assessment procedures to maximize learning and intellectual development. By incorporating evidence-based teaching strategies, such as differentiated instruction, customized learning, and inquiry-based approaches, educators can effectively cater to their students' various learning styles and capacities. Motivation and engagement can be enhanced by providing students with meaningful and relevant learning experiences connected to their interests, prior knowledge, and real-world contexts. Providing chances for active learning, critical thinking, problem-solving, and creativity fosters profound comprehension and advanced cognitive abilities. Furthermore, ensuring that tests align with the intended learning outcomes, offering prompt feedback, and cultivating an environment that encourages introspection and self-evaluation enhance metacognitive awareness and *ongoing progress.*

To summarize, creating ideal learning conditions necessitates a comprehensive strategy that encompasses the physical, social, emotional, and cognitive aspects of learning. By establishing nurturing, all-encompassing, and captivating settings, instructors can enable students to achieve their furthest capabilities, cultivate necessary aptitudes for triumph, and evolve into perpetual learners. Investing in establishing ideal learning environments is crucial not just for academic success but also for fostering the comprehensive growth of students and equipping them to excel in an intricate and swiftly evolving world.

Guaranteeing the availability of critical resources

Ensuring the availability of vital resources is crucial for maintaining the efficient operation of organizations, projects, and procedures. Critical resources refer to a diverse array of both physical and non-physical assets, including as materials, equipment, staff, information, finance, and infrastructure, that are essential for accomplishing goals and producing desired results. This essay will examine the significance of ensuring the accessibility of vital resources and techniques for efficient resource management.

Significance of Ensuring Essential Resources:

Ensuring Continuity: Vital resources are necessary to sustain daily operations and perform fundamental organisational functions. Without essential resources, such as materials, equipment, and personnel, productivity and efficiency may be impaired, resulting in delays, disruptions, and inefficiencies.

Meeting Objectives: Essential resources are crucial in attaining organizational objectives, project milestones, and performance benchmarks. Ensuring the accessibility of resources allows teams to carry out tasks, produce results, and meet deadlines efficiently, improving overall performance and achieving success.

Mitigating Risks: Ensuring the availability of essential resources helps reduce the likelihood of risks and uncertainties related to shortages, bottlenecks, or reliance on such resources. Implementing proactive resource planning and allocation strategies reduces the probability of project delays, cost overruns, and quality problems, improving the project's resilience and adaptability.

Critical resources are crucial in maintaining a business's competitiveness as they facilitate innovation, differentiation, and value generation. Organizations can gain a competitive advantage in dynamic contexts by accessing specialized skills, technologies, and strategic assets. This allows them to take advantage of opportunities and effectively meet market needs.

Boosting Stakeholder Confidence: Ensuring the accessibility of vital resources fosters confidence and trust among stakeholders, such as clients, investors, and partners. Effective resource management methods showcase the organization's proficiency, responsibility, and dedication to achieving outcomes, enhancing relationships, and promoting cooperation.

Optimal approaches for efficient allocation and utilization of resources:

Comprehensive Planning: Perform meticulous resource planning and forecasting to determine essential resource needs, predict variations in demand, and effectively distribute resources. Create alternative plans and tactics to deal with possible limitations or resource interruptions.

Resource allocation should be prioritized according to strategic objectives, project priorities, and value-adding activities. Allocate resources to initiatives and tasks that have a significant effect and are crucial to achieving corporate objectives while providing the highest possible value to stakeholders.

Enhanced Utilization: Enhance the utilization of current resources by implementing effective scheduling, resource sharing, and maximizing capacity usage. Deploy tools and technologies to manage, analyze, and optimize resources to detect and efficiently redistribute unused assets.

Cooperative Alliances: Establish strategic alliances and cooperative ventures with suppliers, vendors, and external stakeholders to improve resource availability and access to specialized knowledge and achieve economies of scale. Utilize outsourcing, joint ventures, and strategic alliances to enhance internal capabilities and address resource limitations.

Continuous Improvement: Consistently assess and enhance resource management processes, systems, and practices using feedback, performance measurements, and lessons learned. Cultivate a corporate environment that encourages and supports innovation, flexibility, and the ability to adapt to address shifting resource requirements and changing market conditions effectively.

Invest in enhancing resilience and redundancy in vital resource supply chains to reduce susceptibility to interruptions, such as natural disasters, geopolitical events, or supply chain disruptions. Diversifying suppliers, preserving safety stock, and identifying alternate sourcing possibilities are also advisable to limit risks and ensure uninterrupted operations.

Ensuring the accessibility of vital resources is crucial for achieving organizational success, effective risk management, and the contentment of stakeholders. Organizations can achieve optimal resource usage, improve competitiveness, and maintain long-term development and resilience in a complex and uncertain business environment by employing efficient resource management techniques.

By leveraging technology to augment educational experiences

Utilizing technology to enhance educational experiences is crucial for updating teaching and learning methods, increasing involvement, and equipping students for success in a digital era. Technology provides numerous potential to enhance educational experiences, customize learning, and broaden access to resources and knowledge. This essay will examine the advantages and methods of incorporating technology into education to enhance learning experiences.

Advantages of Technology-Enhanced Educational Experiences:

Increased Engagement: Interactive multimedia tools, instructional games, simulations, and virtual reality (VR) experiences effectively attract students' attention and encourage active learning. Compelling and immersive educational material stimulates students to investigate topics, test ideas, and engage more actively in learning.

Personalized Learning: Adaptive learning platforms, intelligent tutoring systems, and personalized learning paths utilize technology to customize training based on students' unique requirements, preferences, and learning modalities. Technology facilitates personalized learning experiences, allowing students to advance at their speed, receive focused assistance, and attain mastery of subjects with greater efficacy.

Access to Resources and Expertise: Digital libraries, online databases, open educational resources (OER), and educational websites allow students and educators to access extensive collections of information, multimedia content, and learning materials. Technology enhances collaborative learning by enabling students to share knowledge and connect globally, allowing them to discover other viewpoints, cultures, and resources beyond the confines of the traditional classroom.

Interactive Collaboration: Collaborative technologies, video conferencing platforms, and learning management systems (LMS) facilitate real-time collaboration among students, educators, and specialists, regardless of geographical location. Technology facilitates communication, collaboration, and the sharing of knowledge, which in turn encourages cooperative problem-solving, creativity, and innovation among learners.

Data-driven insights refer to educators' use of learning analytics, assessment tools, and data dashboards to gain valuable and practical information about students' progress, performance, and learning practices. By examining data about student engagement, mastery, and obstacles, educators can pinpoint areas that require enhancement, customize instruction, and implement focused interventions to facilitate student learning and achievement.

Methods for using technology to enhance educational experiences:

Pedagogical Integration: Strategically incorporate technology into curriculum design and teaching methods to improve learning outcomes and accomplish educational objectives. Align technology's use with pedagogical approaches, learning objectives, and assessment strategies to ensure its meaningful integration and impact on student learning.

Professional Development: Equip educators with instruction, materials, and assistance to use technology proficiently in their teaching methodologies. Provide educators with professional development opportunities, workshops, and peer mentoring programs to enhance their digital literacy, instructional technology abilities, and confidence in utilizing technology to enhance educational experiences.
Teach pupils about the responsible and ethical utilization of technology, digital citizenship, internet safety, and information literacy skills. Instruct students to critically assess sources, distinguish reliable information from false or misleading content and participate responsibly in online networks.

Universal Design for Learning (UDL) is a framework that aims to make education accessible to all students, regardless of their abilities or learning styles. By incorporating the concepts of Universal Design for Learning (UDL), create educational experiences that are easily accessible, inclusive, and adaptable to the needs of a wide range of learners. Utilize technology tools and features, such as screen readers, text-to-speech, and captioning, to cater to a wide range of learning styles, preferences, and skills.

Promote exploring new ideas and methods and the imaginative utilization of technological tools and platforms to improve educational experiences. Establish an environment that encourages the development of new ideas, taking calculated risks, and constantly improving the use of technology to enhance teaching and learning.

Ultimately, utilizing technology to enhance educational experiences presents significant prospects for revolutionizing learning and equipping students with the necessary knowledge, skills, and competencies for success in the modern era. By deliberately incorporating technology in education, promoting collaboration, and accepting innovation, we can establish dynamic, captivating, and customized learning settings that equip students for the demands and possibilities of an ever more digital and interconnected world.

CHAPTER FOUR

Leadership and Governance

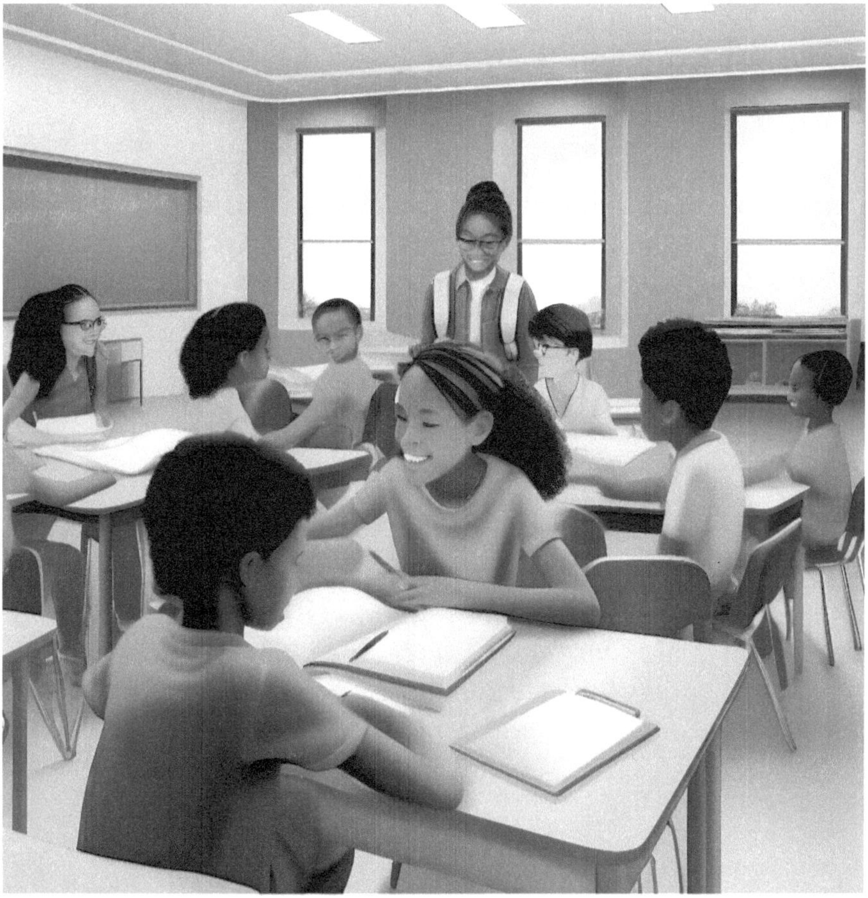

The influence that leadership has on school culture

The impact of leadership on school culture is significant and extensive. It moulds the attitudes, activities, and relationships of all educational community members. School leaders, such as principals, administrators, and department heads, create, foster, and maintain a healthy and inclusive school environment that encourages academic achievement, student welfare, and professional development. This essay will analyze the influence of leadership on school culture and discuss the essential methods for fostering a positive and nurturing educational atmosphere.

Vision and Values: Competent school leaders express a compelling vision and shared values that motivate and direct the school community. Leaders create a shared sense of purpose and direction among stakeholders by establishing clear goals, priorities, and expectations. This develops a collaborative commitment to excellence and ongoing progress.

Ethical leadership promotes trust, honesty, and accountability within the school community. Leaders who exhibit integrity, equity, and openness in their actions and decisions foster confidence and esteem, where individuals feel appreciated, listened to, and empowered to contribute to the school's objectives and aspirations.

Supportive connections: School leaders foster nurturing

connections and establish a sense of inclusion among students, staff, parents, and community members. Leaders cultivate robust relationships and promote a culture of compassion and mutual regard, which improves student well-being and academic achievement through encouraging open communication, collaboration, and empathy.

Instructional Leadership: Competent school leaders prioritise instructional leadership, actively participating in enhancing teaching and learning processes. Leaders enhance teachers' performance and effectiveness by offering instructional assistance, professional development opportunities, and constructive criticism. This empowers teachers to thrive in their professions, deliver high-quality instruction, and effectively address the different needs of students.

Education leaders promote cultural responsiveness by accepting diversity, appreciating inclusivity, and resolving systematic imbalances within the school community. Leaders foster an environment that values, respects, and supports every student in realizing their maximum potential by implementing culturally relevant curricula, inclusive policies, and fair practices.

Collaborative Decision-Making: School leaders cultivate an environment of collective governance and collaborative decision-making, including stakeholders in designing, executing, and assessing school projects and policies. Leaders may foster consensus, ownership, and commitment to group goals and objectives by actively seeking input, considering multiple perspectives, and encouraging participatory decision-making.

Continuous Improvement: Effective leaders are dedicated to constantly improving themselves and acquiring knowledge throughout their lives. They serve as role models by embracing a mindset that values growth, being open to new ideas, and adjusting to evolving demands and situations. Leaders foster a culture of introspection, novelty, and daring, which stimulates originality, adaptability, and ongoing education and enhancement among employees and students.

Ultimately, the impact of leadership on school culture is of utmost importance since it determines the values, norms, and practices that shape the educational experience for all individuals involved. School leaders can create environments where every student excels academically, socially, and emotionally and where educators feel empowered and satisfied in their roles by promoting a positive, inclusive, and supportive school culture based on a shared vision, ethical leadership, supportive relationships, and a dedication to equity and excellence.

Developing inclusive and collaborative leadership practices

Cultivating inclusive and collaborative leadership techniques is crucial to promoting a culture of diversity, equity, and belonging in businesses. Inclusive leadership encompasses various viewpoints, fosters cooperation, and enables every member to utilize their distinct abilities and perspectives to accomplish shared objectives. This essay examines methods for cultivating inclusive and collaborative leadership that advance fairness, stimulate creativity, and improve organizational performance.

Foster Self-Awareness: Inclusive leadership commences with cultivating self-awareness and engaging in introspection. Leaders should critically analyze their biases, preconceptions, and privilege and contemplate how these elements impact their leadership style and decision-making. Through self-awareness, leaders can better understand their strengths and areas for improvement. This enables them to actively foster a more inclusive and fair atmosphere.

Advance Diversity and Inclusion: Inclusive leaders proactively advance diversity and inclusion in their businesses by advocating for equity, impartiality, and representation. They promote inclusive hiring practices, establish platforms for marginalized perspectives to be heard, and cultivate an environment of inclusivity where every individual feels appreciated, esteemed, and integrated.

Trust and psychological safety are essential for effective collaborative leadership in teams and organizations. Leaders should create a conducive atmosphere where individuals feel at ease taking risks, freely sharing ideas, and expressing differing perspectives without fearing retaliation or criticism. Leaders facilitate open communication, innovation, and teamwork by cultivating trust and psychological safety.

Promote Communication and Collaboration: Inclusive leaders promote effective communication and collaboration among various teams and departments. They establish communication channels to facilitate the exchange of information, ideas, and feedback and encourage collaboration across different departments to eliminate barriers and use the combined knowledge and skills inside the organization. By promoting cooperation, leaders effectively utilize the full capabilities of their teams and stimulate innovation and creativity.

Inclusive leaders enhance the capabilities of others by entrusting them with authority, autonomy, and decision-making duties. The organization has confidence in its team members' ability to assume responsibility for their work, use judgment, and make valuable contributions to achieving organizational objectives. Leaders promote the development of ownership and responsibility in others while nurturing a culture that encourages empowerment and progress.

Embrace and Appreciate Feedback: Inclusive leaders proactively seek feedback from their team members, peers, and stakeholders and highly regard various opinions and experiences. They facilitate feedback by regular check-ins, administering surveys, and implementing 360-degree assessments. They then utilize this input to shape their leadership practices and decision-making. Leaders exhibit humility, transparency, and a dedication to ongoing learning and enhancement by actively seeking and appreciating feedback.

Set a positive example: Inclusive leaders demonstrate inclusive attitudes and ideals via their actions and interactions, serving as role models for others. They exhibit respect, empathy, and honesty while interacting with others and take responsibility for supporting the organization's ideals of diversity, equity, and inclusion. Through setting a positive example, leaders foster trust, establish credibility, and cultivate an environment of inclusiveness and collaboration.

Ultimately, it is crucial to cultivate inclusive and collaborative leadership strategies to promote a culture that values diversity, equity, and a sense of belonging in businesses. Leaders can create inclusive and empowering environments for all individuals to contribute their full potential to achieve organizational success by fostering self-awareness, promoting diversity and inclusion, establishing trust and psychological safety, facilitating communication and collaboration, empowering others, valuing feedback, and setting a positive example.

CHAPTER FIVE

Evaluation and Assessment

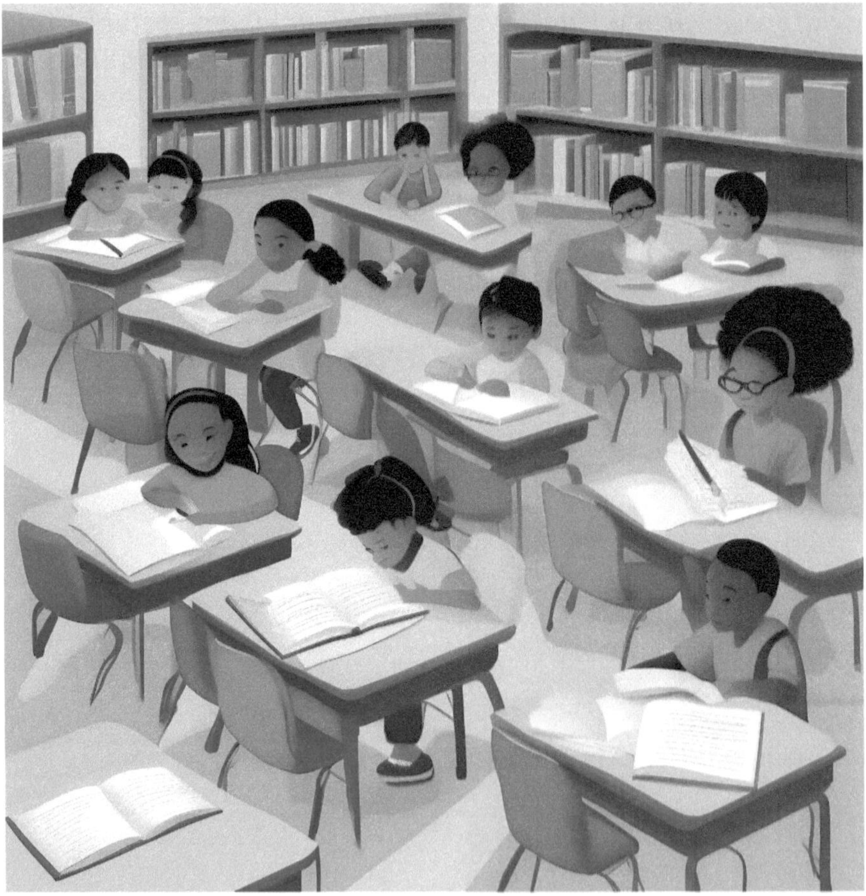

Methods of formative and summative evaluation

Formative and summative evaluations are two separate categories of assessments employed in educational contexts to gauge student learning and advancement. Formative evaluations aim to offer feedback and direct instruction during the learning process. In contrast, summative evaluations evaluate student accomplishment and results after the conclusion of a course, unit, or program. Here are often employed techniques for evaluating both types:

Methods for formative evaluation:

Classroom observation involves teachers monitoring students' behaviour, interactions, and involvement in various class activities, discussions, and group work to evaluate their comprehension, participation, and engagement levels. Observation enables instructors to provide feedback and adapt instruction accordingly promptly.

Questioning tactics: Educators employ many questioning tactics, including posing open-ended inquiries, administering tests, and fostering debates, to assess students' comprehension and develop critical thinking skills. Interrogating promotes engaged involvement and aids in identifying misunderstandings or topics requiring additional explanation.

Exit Tickets or Quick Checks are assessments delivered after a course or class to evaluate students' understanding and recall of essential subjects. These evaluations offer prompt feedback to students and teachers and guide instructional choices for future classes.

Peer and self-assessment activities promote students' introspection regarding their learning and enable them to offer constructive criticism to their classmates. Peer review of assignments, group projects, or presentations enables students to assess and provide constructive criticism of each other's work, fostering collaborative learning and self-reflection.

Teachers continuously provide formative input on student assignments, homework, and projects throughout the learning process. Feedback is characterized by its specificity, actionability, and focus on areas that require improvement. It aids students in comprehending their strengths and limitations and directs their learning progress.

Methods for doing summative evaluations:

Standardized tests, such as state assessments, end-of-course exams, or standardized achievement tests, are given at the end of a course, grade level, or academic year to evaluate how well students have mastered specific subjects or abilities. These assessments offer a uniform gauge of student performance and are frequently employed to ensure responsibility.

Final exams or assessments are comprehensive evaluations conducted after a course or academic term to assess students' knowledge acquisition and proficiency in course material. These examinations encompass many subjects or concepts taught throughout the course and are usually assessed to ensure responsibility and for academic reporting purposes.

Performance-Based exams: Performance-based exams, such as presentations, projects, portfolios, or performances, necessitate students to exhibit their knowledge, skills, and talents in genuine, real-world situations. These examinations evaluate cognitive abilities, innovative thinking, and problem-solving aptitude, comprehensively evaluating student performance.

Rubrics and grading criteria are employed to methodically and consistently assess student work concerning predetermined learning objectives or standards. Rubrics delineate precise criteria and levels of performance for evaluation, offering transparency and clarity in grading and assuring equity and dependability in assessment.

Course evaluations are conducted after a course to collect feedback from students regarding their learning experiences, course content, and the quality of the teaching. These assessments offer instructors sound knowledge to contemplate teaching methodologies and implement enhancements for upcoming courses.

Through diverse formative and summative assessment techniques, instructors can thoroughly evaluate student learning, offer prompt comments for enhancement, and successfully gauge overall achievement and outcomes. These evaluations provide information for making decisions about instruction, directing the development of educational programs, and facilitating ongoing enhancements in teaching and learning methods.

CHAPTER SIX

Student Support Services

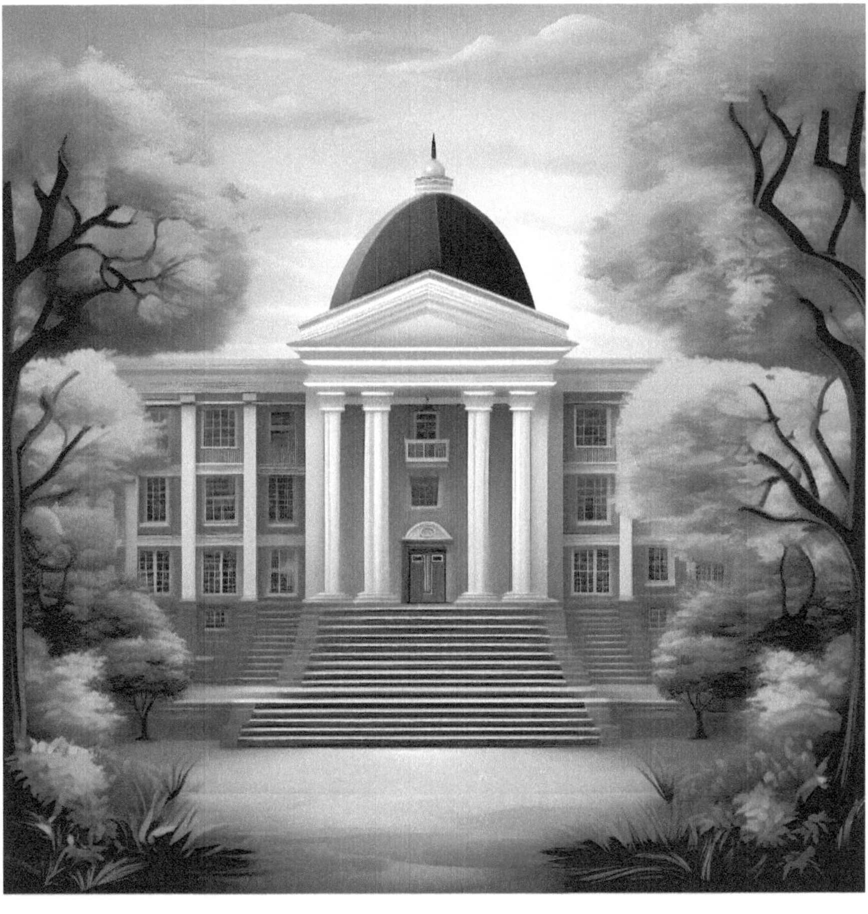

Advancing the comprehensive welfare of students

Advancing students' comprehensive welfare is a multifaceted endeavour that requires a holistic approach to addressing their academic, social, emotional, physical, and mental well-being. By prioritizing students' holistic development, educational institutions can create supportive environments that foster academic success, personal growth, and overall well-being.

Here are key strategies for advancing the comprehensive welfare of students:

Promoting Physical Health and Wellness:

Provide access to nutritious meals, physical activity, and health education programs to promote healthy lifestyles and prevent chronic diseases.

Implement policies and practices prioritising student safety, including measures to prevent bullying, violence, and substance abuse.

Offer health services, counselling, and support for students with chronic health conditions or disabilities to ensure their well-being and inclusion in school activities.

Supporting Social and Emotional Development:

Implement social-emotional learning (SEL) programs that teach students essential self-awareness, self-management, empathy, and relationship-building skills.

Provide counselling services, peer support groups, and mental health resources to address students' social and emotional needs, including stress, anxiety, depression, and trauma.

Create a positive school climate and culture that promotes inclusivity, respect, and empathy, fostering a sense of belonging and connectedness among students and staff.

Fostering Academic Success and Achievement:

Implement evidence-based instructional practices and personalized learning approaches to meet students' diverse needs and learning styles.

Provide academic support services, tutoring, and enrichment programs to help students succeed academically and reach their full potential.

Set high expectations for student achievement while providing the necessary support and resources to help students meet and exceed those expectations.

Ensuring Equity and Access:

Address systemic barriers and inequities that impact students' access to educational opportunities, resources, and support services.

Implement policies and practices that promote diversity, equity, and inclusion, including culturally responsive teaching, anti-bias education, and inclusive curriculum development.

Provide targeted support and interventions for marginalized and underserved student populations, including students from low-income backgrounds, students with disabilities, English language learners, and students from historically marginalized communities.

Building Strong Family and Community Partnerships:

Engage families and caregivers as partners in their children's education, providing opportunities for involvement, communication, and collaboration.

Forge partnerships with community organizations, businesses, and agencies to provide additional resources and support services for students and families.

To foster a sense of social responsibility and citizenship, create opportunities for students to participate in community service, civic engagement, and service-learning projects.

Promoting Career and College Readiness:

Provide career exploration, guidance, and experiential learning opportunities to help students identify their interests, strengths, and career goals.

Offer college preparatory programs, college admissions support, and financial aid assistance to ensure students can access post-secondary education and career pathways.

Foster 21st-century skills such as critical thinking, communication, collaboration, and creativity to prepare students for success in the workforce and society.

By implementing these strategies and prioritizing the comprehensive welfare of students, educational institutions can create environments where all students feel safe, supported, and empowered to thrive academically, socially, and emotionally. Investing in students' holistic development promotes individual well-being and contributes to a more equitable, inclusive, and prosperous society.

Promote constructive teacher-student relationships.

COMMUNITY ENGAGEMENT AND PARTNERSHIPS

The significance of stakeholder involvement in educational initiatives

Stakeholder engagement is crucial for the achievement and long-term viability of educational projects. Stakeholders, such as students, parents, educators, administrators, community members, and lawmakers, significantly influence the course, execution, and results of educational initiatives and reforms.

Here are a few crucial factors that emphasize the need for stakeholder participation in educational initiatives:

Comprehending Varied Viewpoints: Stakeholders provide various viewpoints, experiences, and ideas to the discussion. Engaging stakeholders guarantees that all parties' requirements, worries, and ambitions are considered during the decision-making process. By comprehending a range of perspectives, educational endeavours can become more inclusive, adaptable, and efficient in addressing the requirements of the entire school community.

Establishing Trust and Collaboration: The active participation of stakeholders promotes trust, openness, and cooperation among all individuals engaged in educational endeavours. When stakeholders actively participate in the process of developing, implementing, and evaluating programs, they feel highly regarded and treated with esteem. This cooperative method fosters a sense of collective responsibility, liability, and dedication to achieving endeavours, resulting in more robust connections and enduring results.

Improving Relevance and Effectiveness: To ensure that educational programs are relevant and effective, it is crucial to obtain input from stakeholders. By engaging stakeholders in decision-making, programs can be customized to tackle unique difficulties, use local resources, and take advantage of possibilities. Adopting a participative approach increases the chances of projects aligning with the needs and objectives of the school community, resulting in a bigger impact and higher chances of success.

Advancing Equity and Inclusion: The active participation of stakeholders is crucial for advancing equity and inclusion in education. Involving individuals with many backgrounds and perspectives aids in recognizing and resolving structural obstacles, discrepancies, and inequalities in the availability of resources and opportunities. Through the active participation of marginalized and underrepresented groups in decision-making, educational efforts can achieve more equity, enabling all students to flourish and succeed.

Advocating for Sustainability and Longevity: Achieving sustainable change necessitates obtaining the endorsement and assistance of stakeholders at every hierarchical level. Engaging stakeholders in the process of designing and executing initiatives cultivates a feeling of responsibility and commitment to the results. Stakeholder engagement establishes a basis for sustainability since it increases the likelihood that efforts will be welcomed, adjusted, and maintained over time despite changes in leadership and circumstances.

Promoting and fostering innovation and creativity: Involving stakeholders fosters innovation and creativity in educational activities. By amalgamating a range of viewpoints and specialized knowledge, stakeholders can produce novel concepts, examine alternative methods, and engage in experimental endeavours to address intricate problems. This cooperative problem-solving procedure cultivates a climate of ingenuity, adaptability, and ongoing enhancement in education.

Ultimately, the active participation of stakeholders is crucial for facilitating significant and enduring transformation in the field of education. By involving key individuals and groups in the process of making decisions, establishing trust and cooperation, improving the importance and effectiveness, advocating for fairness and inclusivity, promoting long-term viability, and fostering originality and ingenuity, educational initiatives can become more adaptable, influential, and triumphant in accomplishing their aims and objectives.

Parental involvement in education is to be increased.

Enhancing parental engagement in education is essential for cultivating student achievement, fortifying school communities, and advancing favourable results for all parties involved. Parental participation refers to a broad array of activities and approaches that actively involve parents and caregivers in their children's education, both at home and school. Parental engagement is crucial for several reasons. Firstly, it enhances academic achievement and success in students. Secondly, it promotes positive behaviour and reduces the likelihood of engaging in risky behaviours. Additionally, parental involvement fosters a strong parent-child relationship and improves communication between parents and teachers. To achieve this goal, tactics such as regular communication with parents, involving them in decision-making processes, and providing resources and support for parents can be implemented.

Improving Academic Performance: Research repeatedly demonstrates that adolescents whose parents actively participate in their education tend to have higher academic results, exhibit better attendance, and display improved behaviour in school. When parents actively participate in their children's education, they can offer assistance, motivation, and materials to enhance their academic achievements.

Plan: Create consistent channels of communication between educators and parents, such as newsletters, emails, phone calls, or parent-teacher conferences, to update parents on their children's progress, assignments, and academic requirements.

Encouraging Positive School Climate: Parental engagement enhances a positive school environment by cultivating a feeling of alliance, confidence, and cooperation between educational institutions and families. When parents actively participate in school activities and events, they develop a stronger sense of connection to the school community and are more inclined to support its mission and values.

Approach: Establish avenues for parental involvement in school functions, committees, and volunteer endeavours, such as parent-teacher associations (PTAs), school fundraisers, cultural festivities, and educational programs.

Parental involvement is crucial in fostering students' social and emotional development. It enables parents to offer emotional support, direction, and encouragement to their children, thereby assisting them in overcoming obstacles, fostering resilience, and cultivating healthy connections.

Approach: Provide parenting classes, support groups, and resources focusing on child development, positive discipline, and communication skills. These initiatives aim to enhance parents' abilities in raising their children and foster healthy socio-emotional growth.

Enhancing Equity and Inclusion: Augmenting parental participation can effectively narrow the divide between home and school, especially for marginalized and underserved communities. By involving parents from diverse backgrounds, schools can guarantee that all families experience a sense of acceptance, appreciation, and integration within the educational system.

Approach: Incorporate culturally sensitive methods and proactive initiatives to involve parents from various cultural, linguistic, and socioeconomic backgrounds. Offer linguistic interpretation services, translate materials, and provide culturally appropriate programming to cater to the needs of all families.

Enhancing Parental Advocacy: Parental participation enables parents to actively support and defend their children's educational needs and rights. When parents are knowledgeable, involved, and empowered, they can successfully interact with educators, administrators, and lawmakers to resolve problems, advocate for resources, and promote good change in schools and communities.

Approach: Offer parent leadership and advocacy training programs that teach parents about education policy, school governance structures, and effective tactics for advocating their interests. Encourage parental engagement by encouraging them to express their viewpoints, share their personal experiences, and actively participate in decision-making procedures that impact their children's education.

Enhancing parental engagement in education is crucial for advancing student achievement, establishing resilient school communities, and cultivating a climate of cooperation and synergy between educational institutions and families. By implementing techniques aimed at actively involving parents, schools may provide environments that ensure each kid has the necessary support, resources, and opportunity to excel in their academic, social, and emotional development.

CONTINUOUS PROFESSIONAL DEVELOPMENT

Investing in the development and instruction of educators

Investing in the professional development and training of educators is crucial for raising the quality of teaching, improving student learning outcomes, and expanding the overall efficacy of education systems. Teachers have a crucial impact on students' intellectual, interpersonal, and psychological progress, and engaging in their professional advancement is essential to ensure they possess the necessary expertise, abilities, and materials to address the varied requirements of contemporary learners. Investing in educator development and instruction is crucial for several reasons.

Firstly, it enhances the quality of education by equipping teachers with the necessary skills and knowledge to teach students effectively. Secondly, it promotes professional growth and satisfaction among educators, increasing job performance and retention. Lastly, it fosters a culture of continuous improvement in schools, allowing for the introduction of innovative teaching tactics and the adaptation to evolving educational needs. To successfully implement educator development and instruction, it is recommended to provide ongoing professional development opportunities, establish mentorship programs, and create a supportive and collaborative learning environment.

Enhancing Teaching Excellence:

The quality of teaching plays a crucial role in determining student accomplishment. Investing in the development and training of educators enhances teaching quality by offering chances for professional growth, skill enhancement, and instructional enhancement. Teachers can learn evidence-based methods, cutting-edge teaching methodologies, and efficient classroom management techniques to improve their teaching efficacy and student involvement.

Approach: Provide professional development workshops, seminars, and conferences that specifically target effective teaching and learning methods, personalized instruction, evaluation tactics, and classroom management techniques. Offer continuous coaching, mentorship, and feedback to assist educators in effectively implementing new ideas and improving existing teaching practices.

Addressing the Needs of a Diverse Student Population: Modern classrooms are seeing a growing diversity since they comprise students from different cultural, linguistic, and socioeconomic backgrounds. Investing in the development and instruction of educators enables them to enhance their cultural competence, language proficiency, and inclusive teaching approaches to effectively cater to the needs of all pupils. Educators can learn how to establish culturally sensitive classrooms, adapt teaching methods to individual needs, and assist English language learners, students with impairments, and other varied learners.

Approach: Provide professional growth opportunities centred around culturally responsive teaching, equity and inclusion, trauma-informed methods, and catering to the needs of various learners. Offer tools, techniques, and tactics to assist educators in modifying their teaching methods to cater to the requirements of varied student populations.

Advancing Innovation and Adaptation: Education undergoes continuous transformation, propelled by technological advancements, pedagogical adjustments, and changes in student demographics and requirements. Investing in the development and education of educators fosters creativity and adaptability by motivating them to investigate novel concepts, experiment with cutting-edge methodologies, and adjust their teaching approaches in response to evolving conditions.

Teachers can learn about developing trends, technology, and instructional approaches to remain current and proficient.

Objective: Foster a culture of innovation and ongoing enhancement by promoting educators' involvement in action research, collaborative inquiry, and peer learning communities. Offer educators the chance to investigate novel technologies, instructional tools, and digital resources that facilitate individualized learning, student-centred education, and the development of 21st-century skills.

Ensuring educators' well-being is crucial for their job happiness, professional fulfilment, and ability to stay in the industry. Supporting educators' social, emotional, and mental well-being is integral to investing in their development and instruction. Teachers can learn self-care tactics, stress management approaches, and work-life balance practices to enhance their well-being and resilience.

Approach: Provide wellness programs, mindfulness training, and stress reduction workshops to promote the well-being of educators. Offer educators access to counselling services, employee assistance programs, and peer support networks to aid them in effectively managing stress, dealing with difficulties, and maintaining a harmonious work-life equilibrium.

Developing and enhancing educators' skills and teaching methods promotes the establishment of professional learning communities (PLCs), which facilitate collaboration, the exchange of expertise, and mutual learning among educators. PLCs allow educators to participate in thoughtful analysis, cooperative investigation, and evidence-based decision-making to enhance teaching and learning results.

Plan: Implement Professional Learning Communities (PLCs) in schools or districts to facilitate regular meetings among educators to discuss teaching practices, analyze student data, and collaborate on projects to enhance education. Allocate sufficient time, resources, and support to facilitate Professional Learning Communities (PLCs) in participating in valuable professional development activities, such as lesson study, peer observation, and curriculum development.

Ultimately, allocating resources towards the enhancement and training of educators is crucial for enhancing the calibre of teaching, addressing the varying requirements of students, fostering creativity and flexibility, ensuring the welfare of educators, and establishing communities focused on professional growth. Education systems may boost student learning outcomes, develop a culture of continuous improvement, and prepare students for success in an ever-changing world by equipping educators with the necessary information, skills, and resources to flourish in their practice.

A culture that encourages continuous learning

Cultivating a culture that promotes ongoing learning is vital for firms to adjust, develop, and flourish in the current dynamic environment. An environment that fosters ongoing learning encourages inquisitiveness, a mindset focused on personal development, teamwork, and the ability to bounce back from challenges among staff members. This ultimately results in improved performance, increased innovation, and greater flexibility. Below are several fundamental components of a culture that fosters ongoing learning, along with tactics for nurturing such a culture:

Promote a Growth Mindset: Foster a growth mindset across the organization, wherein employees believe their abilities and intelligence can be enhanced via exertion, repetition, and knowledge acquisition. Motivate employees to adopt challenges, persevere in the face of obstacles, and perceive failures as chances for personal development and knowledge acquisition.

Approach: Offer instruction and materials on the principles and methods of a growth mindset. Identify and commemorate instances of employees who exhibit a growth mentality in their job performance. Promote the practice of supervisors offering constructive comments and providing support to help employees achieve their development and learning objectives.

Encourage Lifelong Learning:

Establish avenues for employees to actively participate in ongoing education and enhance their skills throughout their professional journeys. Provide a range of learning formats and modalities, including workshops, seminars, online courses, mentorship programs, and job rotations, to cater to different learning styles and preferences.

Plan: Implement a comprehensive learning and development initiative that allows employees access to a diverse array of educational materials, such as internal and external training options, financial support for educational expenses, and reimbursement schemes for tuition fees. Promote and support employees in establishing learning objectives and developing customized learning strategies that align with their professional ambitions and the organisation's requirements.

Promote Knowledge Sharing and Cooperation:

Cultivate a culture that emphasizes exchanging knowledge, cooperation, and interdisciplinary learning among teams and departments. Promote and incentivize employees to actively communicate their expertise, best practices, and lessons learned to their colleagues, cultivating a culture of reciprocal assistance and ongoing enhancement.

Plan: Establish formal and informal methods for exchanging knowledge and working together, such as organizing lunch-and-learn events, facilitating brown bag talks, fostering communities of practice, and utilizing internet forums or platforms. Acknowledge and incentivize employees who actively participate in information-sharing and collaborative endeavours.

Set a positive example: Leadership is essential in influencing company culture and establishing a climate that promotes ongoing learning. Leaders should exemplify dedication to ongoing education, inquisitiveness, and receptiveness to novel concepts, motivating staff to adopt a culture of constant enhancement and innovation.

Approach: Foster leaders' engagement in educational and growth endeavours alongside their teams, showcasing their dedication to ongoing learning. Offer leadership development programs that prioritise cultivating a culture centred around continuous learning and innovation inside the firm.

Commend and honour the process of acquiring knowledge and reaching goals: Acknowledge and commemorate educational accomplishments and significant milestones within the organization. Recognize employees dedicated to ongoing education, creativity, and personal development, stressing the importance of lifelong learning as a fundamental business principle.

Strategy: Implement recognition programs or awards to commend employees with outstanding learning outcomes, inventive solutions, or corporate learning and growth contributions. Showcase examples and empirical analyses that exemplify ongoing education's influence on individual and corporate effectiveness.

Fostering a culture that promotes ongoing learning is crucial for firms to adjust, develop, and prosper in the current dynamic and competitive landscape. Organizations can foster an environment conducive to employee empowerment, excellence, and collective success by adopting a growth mindset, promoting lifelong learning, encouraging knowledge sharing and collaboration, leading by example, and celebrating learning achievements.

CHAPTER NINE

PROMOTING INCLUSION AND EQUITY

Resolving disparities in educational equity

Addressing inequalities in educational fairness is an intricate and diverse problem requiring a thorough and systematic approach. Educational equity refers to providing all students with equal access to the necessary resources, opportunities, and support systems for success, irrespective of their background, identity, or circumstances. Tackling inequities in educational equality entails recognizing and eliminating obstacles to access, opportunity, and accomplishment while advocating for fairness, inclusivity, and social justice in education. Below are a few crucial tactics for addressing inequities in educational equity:

Identify and Resolve Underlying Factors: Acknowledge and tackle the fundamental reasons behind gaps in educational fairness, such as systemic injustices, institutional prejudices, socioeconomic elements, and structural obstacles that sustain inequality. Perform thorough needs assessments and data analysis to discover gaps in access, attainment, and outcomes among various student populations.

Approach: Create equality task forces or committees to examine data, detect inequalities, and devise focused actions and tactics to tackle the underlying causes of disparity. Work with community partners, stakeholders, and affected populations to jointly develop solutions that specifically target the distinct requirements and difficulties faced by underserved and marginalized groups.

Guarantee Access to High-Quality Education: Guarantee that every student has access to excellent quality education, which includes challenging content, efficient teaching methods, and nurturing learning environments. Ensure equal access to resources, such as highly qualified educators, advanced educational programs, technology, teaching materials, and extracurricular activities, irrespective of pupils' socio-economic status or residential area.

Strategy: Distribute resources and funds fairly, considering students' specific needs. Give priority to investing in schools and districts that serve underprivileged populations. Enact laws and adopt practices that ensure fair resource allocation, decrease the number of students in each class, and enhance the availability of specialized programs and support services for historically marginalized groups.

Advocate for using culturally responsive teaching and learning methods that acknowledge and appreciate every student's varied backgrounds, identities, and experiences. Culturally responsive teaching entails integrating students' cultural, language, and community resources into the curriculum, instruction, and classroom setting to enhance the relevance, engagement, and empowerment of learning.

Approach: Offer educators professional development and training sessions focused on culturally responsive teaching approaches, multicultural education, and anti-bias pedagogy. Promote educators to integrate a wide range of viewpoints, resources, and instructional methods that accurately represent their students' cultural, racial, and linguistic variety.

Alleviate Socioeconomic inequalities: Alleviate socioeconomic inequalities that affect educational fairness by offering supplementary assistance and resources to students from economically disadvantaged backgrounds, students experiencing homelessness, students learning English as a second language, and students with disabilities. Provide necessities such as ensuring access to sufficient food, stable housing, healthcare, and mental health support to establish a favourable learning environment.

Plan: Introduce comprehensive support services, such as community schools, family resource centres, and social-emotional learning programs, to cater to the overall needs of kids and families. Engage in partnerships with community-based groups, government agencies, and charities to offer various supports and services that target the root causes of socioeconomic inequality.

Enhance Student Voice and Agency: Enable students to act as catalysts for correcting inequalities in educational equity. Facilitate avenues for student leadership, advocacy, and engagement in the decision-making procedures that impact their education. Enhance the influence of students' opinions, viewpoints, and personal encounters to shape policies, strategies, and endeavours that strive to advance fairness and societal equality in education.

Approach: Implement student advisory councils, equity committees, or student-led advocacy groups to actively involve students in recognizing and resolving disparities within their educational institutions and localities. Establish forums that enable students to express their narratives, concepts, and suggestions for enhancing educational fairness and cultivating an atmosphere of inclusivity and belonging.

Promote Collaboration and Accountability: Encourage collaboration among many stakeholders, such as educators, administrators, policymakers, families, community members, and activists, to tackle inequalities in educational equity collaboratively. Implement systems to ensure responsibility and openness to monitor advancements, evaluate results, and enforce the obligations of all parties involved in promoting equity objectives.

Approach: Establish equity teams or task forces consisting of various individuals involved in developing, executing, and overseeing equity initiatives and action plans. Create benchmarks, indicators, and metrics to monitor progress and assess the effectiveness of measures in reducing inequities in educational equity.

Consistently update stakeholders on progress and results and actively seek their input to enhance ongoing development.

To effectively address differences in educational equality, a focused and collaborative effort must be made to tackle systemic imbalances, foster fairness and inclusion, and empower all students to achieve success.

Through the identification and resolution of underlying causes of inequalities, the provision of accessible and excellent education, the promotion of culturally sensitive teaching and learning, the addressing of socioeconomic disparities, the empowerment of student voice and autonomy, and the cultivation of collaboration and accountability, stakeholders can collaborate to establish a fair and impartial education system that caters to the needs of all students, irrespective of their background or circumstances.

CHAPTER TEN

CASE STUDIES AND BEST PRACTICES

Case studies and exemplars of pedagogy at educational institutions offer valuable perspectives and illustrations of successful teaching methods, classroom control methodologies, and student-focused approaches that foster active participation, knowledge acquisition, and scholastic achievement. Presented here are a selection of case studies and best practices that exemplify outstanding teaching methods in educational institutions:

Project-Based Learning (PBL): Case Study: A high school science teacher used a project-based learning methodology to educate students on environmental sustainability. Students collaborate in teams to investigate ecological concerns, conduct scientific investigations, and devise resolutions to practical challenges. The teacher assumes the role of a facilitator, offering advice, comments, and tools to promote student inquiry and collaboration.

Optimal methodology: Integrate genuine, experiential assignments that enable students to investigate intricate subjects, cultivate analytical reasoning abilities, and employ information in practical situations. Facilitate avenues for student autonomy, expression, and innovation in the planning and execution of projects.

Differentiated education: Case Study: A middle school math teacher uses differentiated education to address the varying requirements of kids in her classroom. She builds adaptable learning clusters according to students' preparedness levels, preferences, and cognitive approaches. Students are provided with customized education, activities, and assessments specifically designed to meet their unique needs and strengths.

Optimal approach: Enhance training by offering diverse avenues for learning, such as tiered tasks, adaptable grouping, and diverse instructional materials and tools. Utilize formative assessment data to guide instructional decisions and adapt teaching tactics to cater to the requirements of every learner.

Culturally Responsive Teaching: Case Study: A primary school educator integrates culturally responsive teaching methodologies into her literacy pedagogy. She chooses a variety of texts and literature that accurately represent her students' cultural backgrounds and identities. She integrates multicultural viewpoints, experiences, and customs into classroom discussions and activities to enhance the relevance and inclusivity of learning.

Optimal approach: Incorporate culturally pertinent content, illustrations, and sources into the curriculum to authenticate students' cultural identities and experiences. Cultivate a constructive classroom atmosphere that appreciates diversity, fosters respect, and commemorates cultural distinctions.

Inquiry-Based Learning: Case Study: A secondary school history instructor uses inquiry-based learning to actively include pupils in examining historical events and concepts. Students engage in inquiry by formulating, undertaking investigations, and scrutinizing primary and secondary sources to develop their comprehension of historical events. The teacher fosters discussions, debates, and presentations to promote critical thinking and historical investigation.

Optimal approach: Promote inquisitiveness, exploration, and examination by organizing classes around open-ended inquiries and activities focused on investigation. Facilitate avenues for students to actively participate in research, analysis, and synthesis of knowledge to cultivate a more profound comprehension and admiration for academic subject matter.

Student-Centred Instruction: A Case Study: A secondary English teacher uses a flipped classroom model to employ student-centred learning. Students see instructional videos and complete readings outside of class and then participate in collaborative conversations, group activities, and project-based learning during class. The instructor assumes the role of a facilitator, guiding students in their pursuit of inquiry, discovery, and reflection.

Optimal approach: Transition the emphasis of teaching from being teacher-driven to student-centred by enabling students to assume responsibility for their learning. Facilitate active learning, problem-solving, and peer collaboration to promote engagement, autonomy, and agency in the learning process.

These case studies and best practices illustrate the significance of implementing cutting-edge, evidence-based instructional methods that enhance student involvement, analytical thinking, and academic success.

By integrating these methods into classroom teaching, educators may establish vibrant, all-encompassing learning environments that cater to every student's varied requirements and provide them with the necessary skills for achievement in both academic and non-academic settings.

CHAPTER ELEVEN

Quality Practices Towards School Management

Strategic planning, leadership, resource management, and a supportive learning environment are all essential components of a good school administration strategy.

These strategies for running a school are as follows:

1.

Create a compelling vision and purpose statement that directs all school-related decisions and activities.

2.

Developing and executing a strategy plan with quantifiable objectives and deadlines is known as strategic planning.

3.

Robust Leadership: Develop your ability to lead others and set a good example.

4.

Create a Positive School Culture: Encourage a welcoming and inclusive learning environment.

5.

Professional Development: Make a consistent investment in the continuing education of educators and personnel.

6.

Effective Communication: Keep lines of communication open and honest with parents, teachers, and students.

7.

Data-Driven Decision Making: Monitor and analyze data to guide decisions and assess progress.

8.

Resource Management: Handle funds, space, and technology efficiently in schools.

9.

Development of the Curriculum: Ensure the curriculum complies with student needs and educational requirements.

10.

Supporting educators in applying successful teaching strategies is known as instructional leadership.

11.

Student-centred learning aims to address each student's unique set of needs.

12.

Inclusive practices: Encourage fairness and inclusivity in all school-related endeavours.

13.

Behaviour Management: Use effective behaviour management techniques to keep a happy learning environment.

14.

Student Support Services: Offer all-encompassing assistance, encompassing special education and counselling.

15.

Parental Involvement: Promote and enable parents to participate actively in school activities.

16.

Engagement with the Community: Form solid alliances with stakeholders and the local community.

17.

Frequent Evaluations: Regularly administer formative and summative evaluations to track students' development.

18.

Activities Outside of the Classroom: Provide a range of extracurricular activities to foster student growth and involvement.

19.

Make sure the educational atmosphere is both safe and secure.

20.

Effectively incorporate technology into the processes of teaching and learning.

21.

Student Voice: Provide pupils with a say in decisions made at school.

22.

Innovation: Promote an inventive and creative culture.

23.

Dispute settlement: Put into practice practical dispute settlement techniques.

24.

Promote health and wellness initiatives for employees and students.

25.

Integrate sustainable techniques into the way schools are run.

26.

Acknowledging and Honoring Success: Honor the accomplishments of both faculty and staff.

27.

Transparent Policies: Provide lucid, unambiguous policies for the school.

28.

Frequent input: Request and give staff, students, and parents input regularly.

29.

Maintaining a commitment to ongoing enhancements in every facet of school administration is imperative.

30.

Create professional learning networks so educators can exchange ideas and work together on best practices.

31.

Leadership Development: Help employees and students acquire effective leadership techniques.

32.

Respect for Diversity and Cultural Competence: Encourage both.

33.

Efficient Use of Time: To maximize productivity, schedule and manage your time well.

34.

Collaboration: Encourage cooperation amongst the community, teachers, and students.

35.

Resource Distribution: Ascertain fair distribution of resources to assist every student.

36.

Establish and share with staff and students specific, attainable goals.

37.

Monitoring Progress: Keep a close eye on and regularly assess your goals' progress.

38.

Promote Innovation: Promote creative ideas and approaches to education.

39.

Establishment of Mentorship Programs: Provide staff and students with mentorship opportunities.

40.

Wellness Programs: Implement wellness initiatives to assist students' mental and physical well-being.

41.

Civic engagement and community service should be encouraged.

42.

Transparent Finances: Continue to handle and report finances transparently.

43.

Getting Used to Change: Adjust and react quickly to obstacles and changes.

44.

Developing Relationships: Create a solid foundation of goodwill among the students and faculty.

45.

Student involvement: Use techniques that can boost students' motivation and involvement.

46.

Positive reinforcement is a useful tool for promoting desirable behaviours.

47.

Concentrate on Outcomes: Give your full attention to attaining measurable goals.

48.

Risk management: Put risk management techniques into practice to help reduce possible problems.

49.

Encourage an environment where everyone in the school community is always learning.

50.

Promote reflective practices among educators and administrators to continuously enhance instruction and administrative techniques. Using these tactics, educators may establish a positive school culture and a well-managed, productive learning environment that encourages student success.

About The Author

Dheeraj Mehrotra, MS, MPhil, PhD (Education Management)., a white and a yellow belt in SIX SIGMA, a Certified NLP Business Diploma holder, is an Educational Innovator, Author, with expertise in Six Sigma In

Education, Academic Audits, Neuro-Linguistic Programming (NLP), Total Quality Management In Education, an Experiential Educator, a CBSE Resource towards School Assessment (SQAA), CCE, JIT, Five S, and KAIZEN. He has authored over 100 books on computer science, AI, digital body language, NLP, quality circles, school management, classroom effectiveness, and safety and security. A former Principal at De Indian Public School, New Delhi, (INDIA), NPS International School, Guwahati, and Education Officer at GEMS, Gurgaon, with ample teaching experience of over Three Decades, he is a certified Trainer for Quality Circles/ TQM in Education and QCI Standards for School Accreditation/ School Audits and Management. He has also been honoured with the President of India's National Teacher Award in 2006 and the Best Science Teacher State Award (By the Ministry of Science and Technology, State of UP), Innovation in Education for his inception of Six Sigma In Education by Education Watch, New Delhi and Education World- Best Teacher Award, BOLT Learner Teacher Award by Air India, 'Innovation in Education Award 2016' by Higher Education Forum (HEF), Gujarat Chapter, among others. He has developed over 150 FREE EDUCATIONAL MOBILE Apps for the Google Play Store exclusively for Teachers, Students, and Parents. This work has been recognised by the LIMCA BOOK OF RECORDS and INDIA BOOK OF RECORDS as the only Indian to draw that feast. As a founder and president of the IoT Society of India, he also promotes Technology Globally. Dr Mehrotra is presently engaged as a PRINCIPAL at KUNWARS GLOBAL SCHOOL, Lucknow, India. He has conducted over 2000 workshops globally on "Excellence In Education" integrated with Total Quality Management and Six Sigma, Technology Integration in Education (TIE), Developing towards being ROCKSTAR TEACHERS, including Cyberspace, Cyber Security, Classroom Management, School Leadership & Management, and Innovative teaching within classrooms via Mind Maps, NLP and Experiential Learning in Academics. He is an active TEDx speaker and can be viewed on the YouTube TEDx channel. As a premium UDEMY Instructor, he has developed over 450 courses and caters to over 8 Lakh students from 180 countries. He can be visited at www.authordheerajmehrotra.com

Dr Dheeraj Mehrotra

Robotics
&
Artificial
Intelligence

For ICSE (Class IX)

UNDERSTANDING
Early Childhood
Care And
Education
Dr Dheeraj Mehrotra
Dr Masuda Yasmin

Naturalistic
Intelligence
Among
School Kids
Dr Dheeraj Mehrotra

OPTIMAL
CHILD
DEVELOPMENT

100 Tips For Parents

DR DHEERAJ MEHROTRA

Available at Amazon! Globally!!

Qr Code Video Online

Mastering School Management by Dr Dheeraj Mehrotra, National Awardee Educator, India

இருளில் ஒளி

அரவிந்த் குமார்

(Translated by Smt. Lakshmi)

ISBN 979-8-89446-340-7

சமர்ப்பணம்

என் முதல் புனிதமான ஆசிரியை மற்றும்
என் எண்ணங்களுக்குக் காரணமாக
இருக்கும் என்
அம்மாவுக்கு!

முன்னுரை

பேச்சாற்றல் அற்ற அரவிந்த் குமார் என்ற இளைஞன் சமூக விதிகளை மீறி வழக்கத்திற்கு மாறாக தானே கற்றுக் கொண்டு சிறு வயதிலிருந்தே கம்ப்யூட்டர் கீ போர்டில் டைப் செய்து தன் எண்ணங்களை எங்களுடன் பகிர்ந்து வந்தான்.

முறையான கல்வி இல்லாத போதும் அவனது ஆங்கில மொழிப் புலமை மற்றும் கணக்கீட்டுத் திறன் அபாரமாக இருக்கும்.

அவன் தன் எழுத்தின் மூலம் பலதரப்பட்ட விஷயங்களைப் பகிர்ந்து வந்தான்.

அவன் தனது ஆறாவது வயதிலிருந்தே இத் திறமையை வெளிப்படுத்தினான் என்றாலும் அவன் டைப் செய்யும் போது, அவனைத் தூண்டிவிட அவன் கையைத் தொட்டுக் கொண்டிருக்க நான் அருகே இருக்க வேண்டும் என்று எதிர்பார்ப்பான்.

சிறிது நாட்களில் அவன் தோளில் கை வைத்துக் கொண்டிருந்தாலும் டைப் செய்ய ஆரம்பித்தான்.

அவனது எண்ணங்களைத் தொகுத்து"நீட் போர்ட்ரேட்" என்ற ஒரு இதழை 2019ல் வெளியிட்டோம்.

பின், நான் அருகே இல்லாவிட்டாலும் டைப் செய்ய ஆரம்பித்தான். ஆனால், எங்கள் "குருகுலம்" பள்ளியின் ஆசிரியை "மெர்ஸி ஏஞ்சல்" அவர்களுடன் மிகவும் எளிதாக உணர்ந்து பணிபுரிய ஆரம்பித்துள்ளான்.

சிறிது மாதங்களுக்கு முன் பொதுமக்கள் கேட்கும் கேள்விக்குப் பதிலளிக்க விரும்புவதாகச் சொன்னான்.

பல்வேறு வயதுள்ள மற்றும் பல்வேறு கல்வித் தகுதியுடைய பலதரப்பட்டவர்களிடமிருந்து கேள்விகள் பெறப்பட்டன.

அவற்றுக்கு அரவிந்த் அளித்த பதில்களைத்தான் புத்தக வடிவில் கொண்டு வந்துள்ளோம். இப்புத்தகத்துக்கு (தமிழ் மற்றும் ஆங்கிலம்) தலைப்புகளும் அவனே தேர்ந்தெடுத்தான்.

சில மிகச் சாதாரணமான கேள்விகளாக இருக்கும். பல தத்துவார்த்தமாக இருக்கும். எல்லாவற்றுக்கும் பதிலளித்துள்ளான்.

அவனுக்கு ஊக்கமளித்து பதில்களை வாங்கியதில் முக்கிய பங்கு சுப்ரியா அவர்களைச் சாரும். அவர்களுக்கு என் நன்றியைத் தெரிவித்துக் கொள்கிறேன்.

இவனது இம்முயற்சி இவர்களைப் பற்றிய பொதுவான மதிப்பீட்டை உடைத்தெறிவதாக இருக்கலாம். மேலும் இவர்களுக்குத் தகுந்த வாய்ப்புக்களைக் கொடுத்து சமுதாயத்தில் இவர்கள் குறித்த புரிதலையும் வளர்த்துக் கொள்ளத் தூண்டுவதாகவும் இருக்கலாம்.

அரவிந்தின் இப்பயணம் இவர்களுக்கு வாய்ப்பும் சூழ்நிலையும் அமைந்தால் சமுதாயத்திற்கு அவர்களின் பங்களிப்பும் இருக்கும் என்பதைக் காட்டுகிறது.

அரவிந்தனைப் போல் அதே நிலையில் அவனுடன் பயணிக்கும் அவனது நண்பன் "டேனியல் கிறிஸ்டோபர் ஜான்" இப்புத்தகத்தின் அட்டையின் கலை வடிவம் கொடுத்துள்ளான். அவனுக்கும் என் நன்றியை உரித்தாக்குகிறேன்.

அரவிந்தின் எழுத்துக்களை ஊக்குவித்து, பாராட்டி, அதனை மிகச் சரியாக உள் வாங்கிக் கொண்டு அதன் மூலம் மாறாமல் தமிழில் மொழி பெயர்த்திருக்கும் மியூசிக் தெரபிஸ்ட் லெஷ்மி மேடத்திற்கு என் மனமார்ந்த நன்றியைத் தெரிவித்துக் கொள்கிறேன்.

இப்புத்தகத்தின் மூலம் அரவிந்த் ஒட்டு மொத்த ஆட்டிஸ சமுதாயத்தையும் முன் நிறுத்துகிறான்.

"இருளில் ஒளி" எனும் இப்புத்தகத்தின் மூலம் தன் நேர்மறையான எண்ணங்களை உலகெங்கும் பரப்பி அதன் எல்லையாக குணமளிக்க முயன்றுள்ளான்.

அன்புடன்

ராதா நந்தகுமார் (அரவிந்தின் அம்மா)

இருளில் ஒளி

உங்களைப் போல் ஒரு நேர்த்தியான ஓவியம் மேடையில் வெளியிட்டால் என்ன செய்வீர்கள்?

அதனை விரும்புவது போல நடிப்பேன்.

உங்களால் ஈர்க்கப் படுபவருக்கு உங்கள் அறிவுரை என்ன?

நல்ல விஷயங்களில் பேரார்வம்.

நட்பு குறித்து தங்களது கருத்து என்ன?

உண்மையான நண்பன் எப்போதும் முதுகில் குத்த மாட்டான்.

தங்களை மிகவும் கவர்வது எது?

முதலில் அன்பு!

தங்களை தன்னிறைவு பெற்றது போல உணர வைப்பது எது?

அன்பான சமுதாயம்.

நம் நாட்டைக் குறித்து தங்களுக்குக் கோபம் எதில் ஏற்படுகிறது?

கற்பழிப்பவர்கள் அதிகரிப்பு குறித்து!

நீங்கள் எளிதாக உணர்கிறீர்களா?

ஒவ்வொரு முறையும் எதிர்பார்ப்பு என்னைக் காயத்துக்குள்ளாக்குகிறது. சமுதாயத் தீர்மானம் என்ற வரைமுறைக்குள் வராத வரை நான் எப்போதும் எளிதாகவே உணர்கிறேன்.

எதைப் பயிற்சி செய்ய நான் விரும்ப வேண்டும்?

விடாமுயற்சியில் உறுதி பெற.

மனிதனை எதை வைத்து மதிப்பீடு செய்ய வேண்டும்?

அவனது பொறுமை, சகிப்புத் தன்மை!

போதை குறித்து தங்கள் பார்வை?

பழகிப் போன அந்நடத்தை வாழ்நாளில் தொடரும்.

விவசாயம் குறித்த தங்கள் கருத்து என்ன?

விவசாயம் இந்தியாவின் முதுகெலும்பு!

பள்ளிகள் கற்பனைத் திறனை கொன்று விடுகிறதா?

முற்றிலும் உண்மை.

**குருகுலத்திலிருந்து யாராவது டெட்
டாக்கில் (Ted talk) கலந்து கொள்ள
நீங்கள் விரும்பினால், எதைக் குறித்து
அவர்கள் பேச வேண்டும்?**

கட்டாய நடவடிக்கை குறித்து.

நானா அல்லது நான் இல்லையா?

இரண்டுமே கற்பனை!

**ஏன் நீங்கள் இலைகளைக் கிள்ளிக்
கொண்டே இருக்கிறீர்கள்?**

அது உடனே தன்னை உயிர்ப்பித்துக்
கொள்ளும். பச்சையை அதன் ஆழத்தில்
பார்க்கிறேன்.

**தங்களுக்கு கால இயந்திரம்
கிடைத்தால் என்ன செய்வீர்கள்?**

என் எதிர்காலத்திற்குப் பயணம் செய்து
என்னில் நல்லவற்றைப் பார்த்து
நிகழ்காலத்தை மனதில் நிறுத்துவேன்.

மீண்டும் பிறவி கிடைத்தால் எப்படி பிறக்க ஆசைப்படுவீர்கள்?

இன்றைய மனிதனாக.

கர்மா குறித்து தங்கள் கருத்து

யாருடைய வாழ்க்கையிலும் கர்மா இல்லை!

வன்முறையை வெற்றி பெற சிறந்த வழி எது?

வன்முறையா அல்லது மென்முறையா?

ஆசுவாசப் படுத்திக் கொண்டு சூழ்நிலையை ஏற்றுக் கொள்!

கனவு வேலை என்பது ஒருவருக்கு என்ன? உங்களுடையது என்ன?

ஆத்ம திருப்தியான வேலை.

ஒரு கலைக் கூடத்திற்கு எஜமானராக ஆசை!

தாங்கள் வாழ்க்கையில் என்ன கற்றுக் கொள்ள விரும்புகிறீர்கள்?

சிறந்த செவிமடுப்பவராக (கேட்பவராக)

தனியாக இருக்க விரும்புகிறீர்களா அல்லது எல்லோருக்கும் மத்தியில் இருக்க விரும்புகிறீர்களா?

பாரபட்சம் பார்க்காத மக்களுக்கிடையே.

உலகிற்கு குறிப்பாக ஏதாவது சொல்ல விரும்புகிறீர்களா?

வாழ்க்கையை நான் எப்படி உள்ளுணர்கிறேன் என்பது குறித்து.

எந்த ஐந்து புலன்கள் உறுதியானவை? ஏன்?

பார்வைத் திறன்

நாவின் ருசி

தொடு திறன்

உடலின் வலி உணர்தல்

ஆழ்ந்த நுகர்தல் திறன்

தங்களது பார்வைக்கு உற்சாகமளிக்கக் கூடியது எது?

இரவும் தெரு விளக்குகளும்.

இன்றைய இந்திய அரசியல் குறித்த தங்களது கண்ணோட்டம்?

எல்லா இடத்திலும் ஊழல்.

நீரின் முக்கியத்துவம் குறித்து எழுத முடியுமா?

உலகின் அடிப்படைத் தேவை. உலகின் வாழ்வாதாரம்.

**தினமும் எதனை எதிர்பார்த்து
விடிகிறது உங்களுக்கு?**

புதிய விஷயங்களைக் கற்றுக் கொள்ள ஒரு
புதிய தினம்.

**செய்ய வேண்டிய வேலை ஏதும் இல்லை
என்றால் தாங்கள் என்ன செய்வீர்கள்?**

ஏதேனும் செய்ய ஆரம்பிப்பேன்.

**பத்து நிமிடத்தில் என்னவாக ஆக
விரும்புவீர்கள்?**

ஃபேரி டேல் கதையில் வரும் மன்னனாக
விரும்புவேன்.

**எந்த ஒரு விஷயத்தை பயங்கரமாக
உணர்வீர்கள்?**

சுற்றுச்சூழல் நெருக்கடி.

எந்த சதித்திட்டத்தில் தங்களுக்கு நம்பிக்கை உண்டு?

டி.பி. கூப்பரின் சதி.

நவம்பர் 24, 1971ல் டி பி கூப்பர் என்பவன் அமெரிக்காவில் ஒரு விமானத்தைக் கடத்தி பயணிகளிடமிருந்து பணத்தைக் கொள்ளை அடித்து விட்டு இரவில் விமானத்திலிருந்து பாரசூட் மூலம் குதித்துத் தப்பித்து விட்டான்.

இன்று வரை அதன் துப்பு துலங்கவில்லை.

எந்த ஒரு மேலான சக்தியைப் பெற நீங்கள் ஒரு போதும் விரும்புவதில்லை?

மனதைப் படிக்கும் சக்தி.

ஒருவர் நல்ல மனிதர் என்பதை நீங்கள் எதை வைத்து வரையறுப்பீர்கள்?

உதவிக்கரம் நீட்டுபவர்கள்.

உயிருள்ள ஒரு பொருளை
உலகிலிருந்து நீக்க விரும்பினால்
எதுவாக இருக்கும்?

கூட்டம்.

ராமாயணம் புராணமா அல்லது
வரலாறா?

வரலாறு.

லஷ்மணக் கோடு என்பது வாழ்வில்
எதனை பிரதிபலிக்கிறது?

வெறுக்கத்தக்க நடவடிக்கைக்கு வழிவகுக்கும்

ராமனிடமிருந்து நாம் என்ன கற்றுக்
கொள்ள வேண்டும்?

நல்லொழுக்கம்.

லஷ்மணனிடமிருந்து?

வில் திறமை.

சீதாவிடமிருந்து?

கம்பீரமாக இருப்பது

ராவணன் குறித்த தங்கள் கருத்து?

திமிர் பிடித்த இணை.

ஹனுமான் குறித்த பார்வை?

அசைக்கமுடியாத பக்தன்.

ராமாயணத்திலிருந்து எடுத்துக் கொள்ளப் படும் வாழ்க்கைப் பாடம்?

அன்பும் மரியாதையும்!

ராமாயணத்தின் எந்த பாத்திரத்துடன் தங்களை இணைத்துக் கொள்வீர்கள்?

ஹனுமான்

ஏன்?

மீட்பவர்.

**தங்களது பார்வையில் ஞானத்தை
அடைந்தவரின் அறிகுறி என்ன?**

வாழ்க்கையைப் புரட்டிப் போடும்
சம்பவத்தால் உந்தப்பட்டவர்.

வேலையைச் செய்யும் சரியான முறை?

அமைதியாகவும் அடக்கமாகவும்.

முற்றிலும் உண்மைக் காட்சி எது?

உண்மையில் போலியான காட்சி

எது நம்மை நிறுத்துகிறது?

நம் பதட்டமான மனம்.

நம்மால் சேர்ந்து செய்யப் படும் ஒரு செயல் நாம் தனியாக செய்யவே முடியாத அது எது?

வாழ்வின் எதிர் பாராத தருணத்தை மகிழ்ச்சியுடன் அனுபவிப்பேன்.

இறைவனுடன் எப்படி தொடர்பு கொள்வீர்கள்?

புனித ஒளி மூலம்.

நான் உங்களுக்கு எப்படி உதவ முடியும்?

தொடர்பு கொள்வது மூலம்.

ஒவ்வொருவருக்கும் சில குறிக்கோள்கள் இருக்கும். அது நல்லதா? தங்களுக்கு என்ன?

ஒவ்வொருவருக்கும் இருக்கும். எனக்கு

தனியாக வாழ முடியும்!

மனித சமுதாயத்திற்கு விழிப்புணர்வை
பரப்புவது!

ஏதாவது குற்ற உணர்வு உள்ளதா?

என்னுடைய தினசரி வாழ்க்கைக்கு ராதாவை
(அம்மாவை) தொந்தரவு செய்வதில்.

**வாழ்வின் இந்த அத்யாயத்திற்கு
தாங்கள் கொடுக்கும் பெயர் என்ன?**

அழகின் இடையே இழுபறி!

**தங்களது இப்போதைய வாழ்க்கை
கனவாக இருந்தால் விழித்துக் கொள்ள
விரும்புவீர்களா அல்லது கனவிலேயே
இருக்க விரும்புவீர்களா?**

விழித்துக் கொள்ள.

இன்று செய்த ஆரோக்யமற்ற செயல் என்ன?

சில வகுப்புகளிலிருந்து தப்பித்தது.

வாழ்வில் "ஏன்" என்ற கேள்வியின் முக்கியத்துவம்?

தெளிவு ஏற்படுவது அங்கே.

"அன்பு என்பது பகுத்தறியும் நடவடிக்கை மட்டுமே" என்பதன் அர்த்தம் என்ன?

அன்பு செய்யும் செயலை விரைவு படுத்து!

ஏன் மக்கள் அமைதியை தழுவுகிறார்கள்?

ஆர்ப்பாட்டமான விரைவான பதில் அது.

இவை எல்லாம்தான் நான் விரும்பினேனா? ஏதாவது விடுபட்டிருக்கிறதா?" என்பதன் பொருள் உங்களுக்கு என்ன?

வாழ்க்கையில் அர்த்தத்தைத் தொடங்கவும்.

ஒரு மாணவனின் வாழ்வில் ஆசிரியர் எங்கு அதிகாரம் செலுத்துகிறார்?

அவனது பலம் மற்றும் பலவீனத்தில்.

அடிக்கடி ஜன்னலுக்கு வெளியே தாங்கள் எட்டிப் பார்ப்பது என்ன?

புற்கள் அசைவதை.

"ஒருவருக்கொருவர் அன்பு செலுத்துங்கள் இல்லாவிட்டால் அழுகி விடுவீர்கள்" இதன் அர்த்தம் என்ன?

உங்கள் வாழ்வில் அன்பை அனுமதிக்காவிட்டால் கீழ் நிலைக்குத் தள்ளப் படுவீர்கள்.

எதிர்வினை அல்லது பதில் இவற்றில் சிறந்தது எது?ஏன்?

பதிலளிப்பது.

எதிர்வினை பிறரை எப்போதும் காயப் படுத்தும்.

பதிலளிப்பதே மேலானது.

உங்கள் உறவுகளில் யாருக்கு அன்பும் பாதுகாப்பும் அதிக தேவை என்று உணருகிறீர்கள்?

அரவணைக்கும் அன்னைக்கு அதிக அன்பும் பாதுகாப்பும் அவசியம்!

மனிதனின் மிகச் சிறந்த உறுப்பு எது?

மூளையும் வயிறும்.

மோசமான உறுப்பு?

பின் இணைப்பு.

ஒரு குழந்தைக்கு நாம் கற்றுக் கொடுக்கும் மிக முக்கியமான விஷயம் எது?

பொறுப்பு

பிறரையும் தன்னைப் போல் பாவித்தல்!

பொய் சொல்லலாமா?

ஆம்.

அப்படியானால் ஏன்?

பிறரையோ தன்னையோ காத்துக் கொள்ள!

உங்களது முக்கியமான பண்பு என்ன?

பிறர் பரிகசிக்கும் நிலையிலும் தன்னம்பிக்கையோடு இருப்பது.

உங்களை எழுந்து கொள்ள உந்துதலாய் இருப்பது எது?

இன்று எல்லாம் சரியாக இருக்கும் என்ற எண்ணம்!

தோல்வி வாழ்க்கையில் முக்கியமான அங்கமா?

நிச்சயமாக. அது முக்கியமான ஒன்று.

அதனை எப்படி எடுத்துக் கொள்வது?

உண்மையாக ஒத்துக் கொள்ள வேண்டும்.

நாளின் பெரும்பகுதியை எப்படி செலவிடுவீர்கள்?

பகுத்தறிதலில்.

எந்த ஒரு புராண உயிரினம் உங்களை மிகவும் பாதித்தது? ஏன்?

நெஸ்ஸீ என்று அழைக்கப்படும் "லாச் நெஸ் மான்ஸ்டர்" (Loch Ness Monster) எனப்படும் ஒரு நீர் வாழ் உயிரினம்.

ஸ்காட்லாந்தின் நாட்டுப் புறக் கதைகளில் இதனைப் பற்றி அறியலாம்.

நீண்ட கழுத்துடைய பெரிய உயிரினம்.

தனிமையில் உயிர் பிழைத்த உயிரினம்.

எதனைக் கேட்பது உகந்தது இதயத்தையா அல்லது மூளை சொல்வதையா?

இதயம். மூளை எப்போதும் சுயநலவாதி.

உங்களது பங்கு என்ன?

குணப்படுத்துபவர்.

மகாபாரதத்தில் தங்களுக்குப் பிடித்த கதா பாத்திரம்?

சகுனி.

ஏன்?

ஆட்டத்தை மாற்றி அமைப்பவன்.

**உங்களது சுயசரிதை எழுத
விருப்பமுண்டா? அப்படி எனில்
அதற்குப்பெயர் என்ன வைப்பீர்கள்?**

பெரும் பிரச்சினைகளை அனுபவித்துக்
கொண்டு உயிர் பிழைத்திருப்பவன்.

உங்களுக்கு என்ன அதிகம் தெரியும்?

சிந்திப்பது அதிகம். ஆம். அதிகமாக
சிந்திக்கத் தெரியும்!

**ஏதாவது கல்விசார் துறை குறித்து
தாங்கள் கற்க விரும்புவது?**

புவியியல்.

தங்களைப் பொறுத்தவரை, சந்தோஷமாக வாழ்க்கை நடத்த புத்திசாலித்தனமாக இருக்க வேண்டுமா அல்லது உணர்வுபூர்வமாக இருக்க வேண்டுமா?

இரண்டும் வாழ்வின் அடிப்படை.

சூரியன் அதிக வெப்பமாக இருக்கும் போது விண்வெளியில் குளிர்ச்சி ஏன்?

இரண்டும் ஒன்றோடொன்று மோதிக் கொள்வதில்லை.

இந்தியா பெருமைப் பட்டுக் கொள்ள முக்கிய 3 விஷயங்கள் என்ன?

பாரம்பரியத்தின் நாகரீகம்

தொழில்மயமாக்கல்

உணவு தானியம்

ஒரு தலைவரின் மிக முக்கியமான தன்மை என்ன?

சமரசம் செய்து கொள்ளும் பண்பு.

எதனை உடைக்க முடியும் ஆனால் எப்போதும் வைத்திருக்க முடியாது?

தாழ்வு மனப்பான்மை.

மனிதன் தான் என்ன நினைத்தாலும் செய்ய முடியும்? உண்மையா?

ரஷ்யாவைச் சேர்ந்த சிறைக்கைதி 25 நாட்கள் தூங்காமல் உயிர் வாழ்ந்தான்.

நீங்கள் புத்திசாலியாக இருக்கும் போது உலகை மாற்றுவீர்கள் அறிவாளியாக இருக்கும் போது?

ஞானத்தின் அதிகாரத்தை மாற்றுவேன்.

இரண்டு விஷயங்களை நீங்கள் எப்போதும் வைத்துக் கொள்ள ஆசைப் பட்டால் எவை அவை?

இடர் காலத்திலும் தைரியம்

அஞ்சா நெஞ்சம்!

அன்பு என்பது என்ன உணர்வை தங்களுக்கு அளிக்கும்?

நிரந்தரமான சுவாசம்!

கடந்த கால, எதிர் கால, நிகழ் கால நிகழ்வுகளில் எதனைப் பார்க்க விரும்புகிறீர்கள்?

நடுத் தர வயதின் நிகழ்வுகளை.

எதற்கு ஐந்து விரல்கள் உண்டு ஆனால் கை இல்லை?

கையுறை.

ஆபத்து என்பது தங்களைப் பொறுத்தவரை?

சூழ்நிலைகளை எதிர் கொள்வது. வெளிப்படையாகப் பேசுவது.

தேசம் குறித்த நமது கடமை என்ன?

நமது செல்வங்களைப் போற்றிப் பாதுகாப்பது.

கருத்துச் சுதந்திரத்தை யார் அதிகம் தவறாகப் பயன்படுத்துவது?

ஸ்திரத் தன்மை (நடுநிலை) இல்லாதவர்கள்.

கடவுள் மனிதனை ஏன் படைத்தான்?

பெருந்தன்மையைக் காண்பிக்க,

விடுதலை நமக்கு என்ன தருகிறது?

இயற்கையான சுதந்திரம்!

எண்ணங்களில் "ஓம்' காரத்தின் விளைவு?

மூலத்தின் உணர்வு.

பாவத் (ஆன்ம) துடிப்பின் முக்கியத்துவம் என்ன?

ஞானத்தின் நுண்ணறிவு!

உங்கள் தந்தையிடமிருந்து என்ன கற்றீர்கள்?

இணக்கமான தன்மை.

நெருப்பு நமக்கு கற்றுக் கொடுக்கும் பாடம்?

பாவத்தின் தண்டனையாளர்.

மேற்கோள்:

எப்போதும் மகிழ்ச்சியாக இருங்கள்

தகுதி ஒரு போதும் மானியத்தை தீர்மானம் செய்யாது!

உங்களது விசித்திரத் தன்மையை எப்படி எதிர் கொள்வீர்கள்?

மறைக்கப் பட்ட புன்னகையால்!

எந்த ஒரு கலையில் நன்கு தேர்ச்சி பெற விருப்பம்?

உளவியல் டெலிபதி. (ஒருவர் மனதிலிருந்து மற்றொருவர் மனதிற்கு எண்ணங்கள் பரிமாறப்படுவது)

டெல்லியின் உங்கள் அழகிய நினைவு என்ன?

காற்றின் சரிவுகள்

எந்த புராண கதா பாத்திரத்துடன் தங்களை இணைத்துக் கொள்வீர்கள்? ஏன்?

ஹெஸ்டியா. இவள் கிரேக்கப் புராணத்தில் வரும் ஒரு கன்னித் தெய்வம். உலையின் கடவுள்.

அன்பான, சண்டையிடாத, மன்னிக்கக் கூடிய, விவேகமான தெய்வமாய் வர்ணிக்கப் படுபவள்.

உங்கள் வாழ்நாளில் எதனை சேகரிக்க விரும்புகிறீர்கள்?

நிரந்தரமான கணத்தை.

எந்த ஒரு விஷயம் நீங்கள் இனி மறுபடியும் செய்ய மாட்டீர்கள்?

பிறரைக் காயப் படுத்த மாட்டேன்.

உங்கள் நண்பர் யாராக இருக்கலாம்?

மதிப்பீடு செய்யாத உணவுப் பிரியர்.

ஏதாவது கச்சேரி செல்ல விரும்புகிறீர்களா?

கூட்டம் பிடிக்காது.

உங்களது மந்திரம் என்ன?

அமைதி மற்றும் உதவி செய்தல்.

எதிர் காலத்தைக் காட்டும் ஒரு கிரிஸ்டல் பந்து உங்கள் கையில் கிடைத்தால்?

நான் உயிருடன் இருக்கிறேனா என்று பார்ப்பேன்.

ஊக்கமின்மையை எப்படிக் கையாளுகிறீர்கள்?

ஊக்கம் கொடுக்காத மனிதர்களிடமிருந்து விலகி இருந்து.

தலைவனின் பண்புகள்?

சுதந்திரமாகச் செயல் பட வேண்டும்.

நிறைவற்ற தன்மையை எப்படி கையாள்வது?

மனிதரில் நிறைவற்றவர்கள் இல்லை.

நன்றியுணர்வு எவ்வளவு முக்கியம்? நீங்கள் அதனை தினமும் வெளிப் படுத்துகிறீர்களா?

அது முக்கியமானதல்ல ஆரோக்யமானது.

நிச்சயமாக. நான் வெளிப் படுத்துவேன்.

நீங்கள் எதற்கு நன்றியுடன் உள்ளீர்கள்?

உயிரோடு இருப்பதற்காக!

மாற்றத்தைக் கையாள்வது தங்களுக்கு சிரமமா?

ஆம். ஏற்றுக் கொள்வது கடினம்.

வாழ்க்கையில் உண்மையான இணைப்புகளின் பங்கு?

உங்களுடைய பாதிக்க வாய்ப்புள்ள மற்றும் உண்மையான வாழ்க்கைப் போக்கை அவை வெளிக் கொணர வேண்டும்.

உங்களைப் பொறுத்தவரை பெண்கள் வளர்த்துக் கொள்ள வேண்டிய மிக முக்கிய பண்பு என்ன?

வளர்த்துக் கொள்ளத் தேவை இல்லை. முதலில் அவர்களது மன நிலை ஊசலாட்டத்தைக் (*mood swing*) கட்டுப் படுத்தவும்.

உணர்ச்சிகளை எவ்வாறு பார்த்துக் கொள்ள வேண்டும்?

அதில் கவனம் செலுத்தாமல் இருக்க வேண்டும்.

தெய்வீகத் தன்மையை எப்படி காண்கிறீர்கள்?

நலம் மற்றும் பரிசுத்தம் ஆகியவற்றைப் பேணும் போது.

நோக்கத்தை அடையும் பாதையில் எதனை விட வேண்டும்?

விரக்தியைக் கை விட வேண்டும்.

போர் அடிக்கிறது என்றால் என்ன? உங்களுக்கு போர் அடிக்குமா?

இல்லவே இல்லை. நான் எப்போதும் ஏதாவது சிந்தனையில் மூழ்கி இருக்கிறேன்.

மன்னித்தல் எவ்வாறு உதவும்?

மன அமைதிக்கு உதவும்.

தீவிர அனுபவம் என்பது உங்களுக்கு என்ன?

கலந்து கொள்ளாத விவாதம்.

கடந்த கால குற்ற உணர்ச்சியை எப்படி கையாள்வீர்கள்?

மனம் கடந்த காலத்தை அசை போடுவதில் விருப்பமில்லை.

வாழ்வில் மிகக் கடினமானது என்று எதனை நீங்கள் உணர்வீர்கள்?

என்னை மீட்டெடுத்துக் கொள்வது

உணர்விலிருந்து விலகி இருப்பது!

**பிறர் மனதைப் படிக்காமலிருந்தால்
என்ன கிடைக்கும் உங்களுக்கு?**

உற்சாகம் இருக்காது!

**உங்களைக் காயப் படுத்தியவரை
எப்படி கையாள்வீர்கள்?**

ஒரு போதும் காயப் படுத்த மாட்டேன்.

பன்னீரை எதனுடன் இணைக்கலாம்?

அது ஒரு முழுமையான உணவு.

கறுப்பு நிறம் எதனைக் குறிக்கிறது?

வீரத்தை.

மூச்சை ஆழமாக இழுத்து விடும்போது?

பதட்டத்திலிருந்து விடுதலை

இந்தியாவை பாரத் என்று பெயர் மாற்றுவது குறித்து?

நாம் பாரதீயர்கள்தான்.

"கற்றுக் கொண்டு வளர்" என்பதை எப்படி உணர்வீர்கள்?

அது குறிப்பிடத் தக்க ஒன்று.

உங்களைப் பொறுத்தவரை கலங்கரை விளக்கம் என்பது என்ன?

துல்லியமாகக் காட்டுவது.

எதிர்காலத்தில் வாய்ப்பு எதற்கு அதிகம் உள்ளது திறனுக்கா அல்லது திறமைக்கா?

திறனுக்கு.

த்வைதத்திலிருந்து அத்வைதத்திற்கு எப்படி செல்வது?

அத்வைதத்திலேயே நிலைத்து நில்!

எதுவும் நீடித்திருப்பதில்லை.

ஆன்லைன் வகுப்புகளில் என்ன கற்றுக் கொள்கிறோம்?

புத்திசாலித் தனமாக நகர்வதற்கு!

ஒரு மருத்துவரின் மிக முக்கியமான பண்பு?

அமைதியும் சகிப்புத் தன்மையும்!

அறியும் ஆர்வம் நமக்கு எதில் உதவுகிறது?

தவிர்க்க முடியாதது.

அன்பெனும் உணர்ச்சி எப்படி விளக்க முடியும்?

நன்கு பலப் படுத்தப்பட்டது.

வாழ்வில் (multiple choice) பலவகை விருப்பத் தேர்வின் பங்கு என்ன?

இக்கட்டான தேவை.

உங்களைப் பற்றி அபிமானித்து ஏதாவது எழுத முடியுமா?

நான் மற்றவர்களை மதிப்பது அபிமானத்துக்குரியது.

புதியவரிடம் உங்களது மறக்க முடியாத அனுபவம்?

புதியவர்கள் என்னைப் பார்க்கும் போது என்னிடத்தில் அன்பை வெளிப்படுத்துவார்கள்.

**என்ன உரையாடல் மிகவும்
மகிழ்ச்சியைக் கொடுக்கும்?**

கிசுகிசு!

**நம் பாத்திரத்தை நிரப்பும் முன்
பிறருக்கு சக்தியை அளிப்பது எவ்வளவு
முக்கியம்?**

உன் பாத்திரத்தை நிரப்புவதற்கு முன்
பிறருக்கு ஆற்றலைக் கொடு.

**என்ன காரியம் செய்து நீங்கள் பெருமை
அடைந்தீர்கள்?**

எனைக் குறித்து நான் ஒரு போதும் பெருமை
அடைந்ததில்லை.

**இதுவரை உங்கள் உடம்பு உங்களுக்கு
செய்த உதவிக்கு ஒரு லவ் லெட்டர்
எழுதுங்களேன்?**

இந்தக் கூக்குரலோ தற்காலிகமானது

இவ்வுடலோ நகைப்புக்குரியது

வேறு என்ன எனக்கு வேண்டும்?

நான் அன்பில் நிலைத்து இருக்கிறேன்!

கவனிப்பு:

வினையின் வேகம் அதிகரித்தால்

தவறுகள் தவிர்க்க முடியாது

வினை தொல்லை தந்தால்

எதிரிகள் நிச்சயம்

வினை பயங்கரமானால்

அழிவு நிச்சயம்

வினை மிகச் சரியாக இருந்தால்

வெற்றி நிச்சயம்!

இன்றைய மேற்கோள்:

ஒருவர் முயற்சி செய்யாமல் வெற்றியடைய முடியாது!

முயற்சிகள் செய்வதற்கு பொறுமை வேண்டும்!
அனுபவத்தின் பலனே பொறுமை!

ஒருவருக்குக் காலம் இல்லாவிட்டால் அனுபவம் கிடைக்காது!

ஒருவருக்கு வெற்றியை விட மற்றொன்று
மகிழ்ச்சியை கொடுக்காது!

தொடர்வது பாராட்டுக்களும் கைதட்டல்களும்!

மனித மூளையில் விஷ்ணு ஸஹஸ்ர நாமத்தின் விளைவு?

தெய்வீகமான, புனிதமான உணர்வு!

சில உறுப்புகளை கடவுள் இரண்டாகக் கொடுத்துள்ளது குறித்து?

ஆரோக்யத்திற்கு இடமளிக்க!

ஆரஞ்சு நிறம் எதனை நினைவுறுத்துகிறது?

அகண்ட அறிவு!

நமக்கு, கிரகணம் எதனை நினைவு படுத்துகிறது?

விநோதத்தை ஆராய!

எந்த புராணம் அல்லது வரலாறைப் படிக்க விரும்புகிறீர்கள்?

அப்ஃராடைட் குறித்து. (Aphrodite)

இது அன்புடன் தொடர்பு படுத்தப் படும் புராதன கிரேக்கக் கடவுள் ஆகும். கடல், போர் ஆகியவற்றின் பெண் தெய்வமாகவும் வணங்கப் படுபவள்.

ஏன் பகவான் கிருஷ்ணர் குழலூதுகிறார்?

அவருடைய மன மகிழ்ச்சிக்காக!

உத்தவ கீதை தெரியுமா?

தெரியாது.

நம் சொகுசு வாழ்க்கையை எப்படி உடைத்தெறிவது?

புதிதாய்க் கற்றுக் கொள்வதன் மூலம்.

நம் கையிலிருக்கும் ரேகைகளுக்கு அர்த்தம் உண்டா?

எதிர் காலத்தைக் கூறும்.

மேற்கோள்:

அமைதிக்கான நேரங்கள் இயற்றவும்!

மக்கள் மற்றவர்களிடம் கருணை காட்ட வேண்டும்

மனநிலையின் நிலைப்பாடு எப்போதும் முக்கியமானது.

குருவின் வாழ்க்கைத் திட்டம் என்ன?

என் முழு முயற்சியையும் எழுதுவதில் கொடுப்பேன்.

ஏன் கவர்வதற்கு நினைக்கிறீர்கள்?

கவர்வதற்கு அவசியமே இல்லை!

பழைய கர்மாவைக் கழிக்க என்ன செய்ய வேண்டும்?

ஒன்றும் செய்ய வேண்டாம்.

சரணடைதலை எப்படி ஏற்றுக் கொள்வது?

தவறு செய்திருந்தால் சரணடைந்து விடு. அது மன நலனுக்கு நல்ல வழி.

கீர்த்திவாசன் பட்டன் கடிக்கும் பழக்கத்தை எப்படி நிறுத்துவது?

அவனுக்கு அது பழகி விட்டது. பர்பி போல் ஏதாவது கொடுக்கலாம்.

ஏன் தங்களுக்கு ஆழ்ந்த நெடியுள்ள பொருள்கள் பிடிக்கிறது?

அது அவ்வளவு ஆழ்ந்த நெடி இல்லை.

சந்யாஸி குறித்த தங்கள் கருந்து?

நிரந்தரம்!

எப்படி தெளிவு படுத்துவது?

வார்த்தைத் திருப்பம் மூலம்.

மேற்கோள்:

எல்லாமே பரிசுத்தப் படுத்துதல்தான்!

புது வருடம் என்பது?

மகிழ்ச்சி அளிக்கும் ஒரு வருடத்தின் ஆரம்பம்.

உங்களுடைய நிறைவேற்றப்படாத கனவு?

கோவா பயணம்.

ஆன்மீக பயணத்தில் பெரிய சவால்?

மோசமான எண்ணங்களை நிராகரித்தல்.

தங்களைப் பொறுத்தவரை குரு என்பது என்ன?

கண்கவர் கபடமில்லாதவர்.

(அரவிந்த் தன்னை குரு என்று சொல்வதுண்டு)

கடவுளுக்கு அடுத்த நிலையில் இருப்பவர்.

உங்களுடைய குரு யார்?

ராதா நந்தகுமார் (அம்மா)

உங்கள் அப்பாவிடமிருந்து என்ன கற்றுக் கொண்டீர்கள்?

தயக்கமில்லாமல் ஆர்வமுடன் உழைக்கும் கலையை.

உங்கள் வாழ்க்கையில் தாக்கத்தை ஏற்படுத்தியவர்கள் யார்?

சத்குரு, விஜய் நாயர், ஆரோக்யமான மனம் மற்றும் எண்ணங்கள்.

உங்கள் மனதுக்குப் பிடித்த குழந்தைக் கால நினைவு?

அம்மாவிடமிருந்து விண்வெளி குறித்து கேட்ட கதை.

எது தங்களுக்கு மகிழ்ச்சியைக் கொடுக்கும்?

இலக்கியங்களை ஆழ்ந்து சிந்திப்பது

பிறர் குறித்து மகிழ்வது.

முழுமை என்பது என்ன?

மனிதன் முழுமையாய் இருக்க முடியாது!

வீட்டுக்கு வீடு மூவர்ணக் கொடி குறித்து?

ஒவ்வொரு சந்ததியினரின் வீட்டிலும் இருக்க வேண்டும். நிச்சயமாக மனதில் இருந்தாலும் போதும்.

மேற்கோள்:

உங்கள் உணர்ச்சி உங்களது கண்ணியத்தைக் குலைத்திடாமல் பார்த்துக் கொள்ளவும்.

எந்த ஒரு நாளை மறக்காமல் இருக்க விரும்புகிறீர்கள்?

பழைய நினைவில் திளைக்க விரும்புவதில்லை. வருத்தம் ஒன்றும் இல்லை.

வேலையையும் வாழ்க்கையையும் எப்படி சமன் செய்வது?

அமைதியாக இருக்கவும். இரண்டும் எப்போதும் உங்கள் மன நலனைப் பாதிக்காது.

உங்களுக்கு மன அமைதியைத் தருவது?

எளிமையாகப் புரியக் கூடிய சாதாரண விஷயங்கள்.

வாழ்க்கையில் முழுமையாக நிரப்பப்பட்டது குறித்த உங்கள் என்ணம்?

வணிகர் கூட நிரப்ப முடியாது. வாழ்க்கையை வாழ்ந்து பார்.

குழுத் தலைவன் எப்படி இருக்க வேண்டும்?

தவறுக்கு பொறுப்பேற்க வேண்டும்.

பிறருடன் தொடர்பு கொள்ளுதல் உங்களை எவ்விதத்தில் மாற்றுகிறது?

எண்ணங்கள் பரிமாறப் படுகிறது.

உங்கள் கனவு என்ன?

மாற்றுத் திறனாளிகள் அனைவருக்குமான மாறுபட்ட நூலகம் அமைக்க!

நாம் எல்லோரும் எதற்கு நன்றியுணர்வுடன் இருக்க வேண்டும்?

இந்த அழகான உலகத்தை அனுபவிக்க!.

உங்கள் வாழ்வில் ஏதாவது இரண்டாவது முறையாக எதிர் கொள்ள விருப்பமா?

இல்லை. நான் மகிழ்ச்சியாக இருக்கிறேன்.

மேற்கோள்:

எப்போதும் நம்பிக்கையுடன் இரு!

தெய்வீகம் என்பது என்ன?

இனிமையான உள் அமைதி!

நீர் என்பது என்ன உலகுக்கு?

தவிர்க்க முடியாத ஒன்று.

நிச்சயமற்ற தன்மையை எப்படி எதிர் கொள்வது?

உடனடியாக எதிர்கொள்வதில் விருப்பம்

சோகமான தடுமாற்றத்தில் உதவிக் கரம்.

வாழ்வின் சம்பவங்களை நாம் மாற்றி அமைக்க முடியுமா?

நிகழ்காலத்தில் மனதைத் திருப்பவும்.

பிரதிபலிப்புக் கேட்டல் என்பது என்ன?

உள்ளுணர்தலில் நல்ல தேர்ச்சி!

மார்கழி என்பது தங்களுக்கு?

குறைவான வெளிச்சத்துடனான
மகிழ்ச்சியான மாதம்.

விழாக்களில் விளக்குகளின் ஒளி?

எனக்கு அது வகை வகையான உணவுக்கான
நேரம். ஹா ஹா ஹா..

மாறுபட்ட மனங்களைப் படிக்கும் போது என்ன தேடலாம்?

சற்குணங்களை!

அறிவை செயலாக மாற்றுவது எவ்வாறு?

பரந்த நோக்கத்துடனான சிந்தனைகளுடன்.
திறந்த மனதுடன் உள் வாங்கிக் கொள்ளும்
ஆற்றலுடன்.

ஏதாவது அடைய விரும்புகிறீர்களா இப்போது?

விநோதமான மனிதனாகவே எப்போதும் இருப்பதை.

பிறர் வற்புறுத்துவதற்காக ஏதோவொன்றை பெறப் படும் செயலால் ஏற்படும் கோபத்தைப் பிறர் மீது காட்ட முயலும் போது?

புறக்கணிக்கப் படுவாய்.

கவனம் ஈர்க்க விரும்புவரை எப்படி கையாள வேண்டும்?

ஒரு போதும் கவனத்தை அவரிடம் திருப்பாதே.

ஈடுபாடு எதில் முடியும்?

மனதுக்குகந்த பலனைப் பெற!

**நம் வாழ்வில் ஒவ்வொன்றும்
எதிலிருந்து உருவாகிறது?**

ஆழமான பரிணாமத்திலிருந்து.

**வாழ்வில் மேம்படுத்த வேண்டிய
முக்கியமான அங்கம்?**

சகிப்புத் தன்மை!

**நல்லவர்களுக்கு ஏன் கெட்டது
நடக்கிறது?**

எல்லோரும் கடவுளின் கால்அடியில்
இருக்கிறோம். எல்லாமே கடவுளின் சித்தம்!

**மனிதர்களுக்கு எல்லாமே
வரையறுக்கப் பட்டிருக்கிறதா அல்லது
தேர்வு செய்ய சுதந்திரம் உள்ளதா?**

தேர்வு செய்ய சுதந்திரம் உள்ளது.

நாம் மனதைப் படிக்கக் கற்றுக் கொண்டால் மனம் மற்றும் ஆற்றல்களை வெல்கிறோம் என்பது குறித்து?

ஆன்மாவை!

மேற்கோள்:

தண்டனைக்குப் பிராயசித்தம் தேவை!

குருகுலம் ஒரு குறும்படம் எடுத்தால் அதன் கதையை ஒரு வரியில் பகிர்வீர்களா?

பிறகு சொல்கிறேன்.

கிறிஸ்துவத்தில் சிலுவை எதைக் குறிக்கிறது?

மக்களுக்காக பரிசுத்த ஆவி துன்புறுத்தப் படுதல்.

எத்தனை நாளுக்கொரு முறை மனித உடலில் செல்கள் மாறுகின்றன?

தெரியாது.

காய்கறிகளுக்கு ஏன் நிறம் உள்ளது?

அதில் விட்டமின்கள் இருப்பதால்.

இலைகள் ஏன் வெவ்வேறு வடிவங்களில் உள்ளன?

இயற்கையின் மாற்றத்தால்.

ஆன்மீக புத்தகங்கள் தங்களுக்கு என்ன கற்றுக் கொடுக்கிறது?

ஸ்திதப்ரக்யனாக (இன்பம் துன்பம் இரண்டுக்கும் அசையாமல்) இருக்க.

இருளும் ஒளியும் என்பதன் அர்த்தம்?

இன்பமானாலும் துன்பமானாலும் அசையாமல் அமைதியாக இருப்பது!

அன்பு என்பது என்ன?

வெளிப்படுத்த முடியாது.

அமைதி என்றால் என்ன?

உள்ளே ஒரு திருப்தி!

கடவுளுக்கு வடிவம் கொடுப்பது குறித்த தங்கள் கருத்து?

சிற்பத்தில் அன்பைக் காண்பிக்கிறோம்.

மேற்கோள்:

போர் நாடுகளில் போர் நிறுத்தம் மிக அவசியம்.

குறும்படத்திற்கான கதையின் வரி?

விவரிக்க முடியாத ஒரு உள்ளத்தின் கதை!

வலியை எப்படி எதிர் கொள்வது?

வலி எங்கு வருகிறது என்று பார். அதனில் நீடிக்க முடிந்தால் வலியை எதிர் கொள்ளலாம்.

உங்கள் வாழ்க்கையின் விதி என்ன?

அகண்ட விநோதமான எண்ணங்கள் வேண்டும்.

உண்மையின் ஸ்வரூபம் வெளிப்படுமா?

நாடகம் முடிவுக்கு வரும் போது.

விசாரணை என்பது என்ன?

ஆய்வு.

"நாராயண அகிலகுரு பகவன் நமஸ்தே"என்பதன் அர்த்தம் என்ன?

மிதக்கும் அலையின் இடை நிறுத்தம்!

தொடுதல் என்ன உணர்ச்சியைக் கொடுக்கும்?

நல்ல அனுபவம்.

கடவுளை நீங்கள் எப்படிப் பார்க்கிறீர்கள்? உருவத்துடனா? உருவமில்லாமலா?

உருவமில்லாமல்.

அவரிடம் என்ன வேண்ட வேண்டும்?

இக்காற்றில் என் காற்றை நிறுத்தி விடாதே!

மேற்கோள்:

ஆழ்ந்த பார்வை ஆரோக்யமானது.

எது உண்மையான சுதந்திரம்?

மக்கள் மற்றவர்களின் கருத்துக்களால்
புண்படுவதை நிறுத்தும் போது!

சுக போகம் நமை எங்கு கொண்டு விடும்?

இடர்களை எதிர்கொண்டு வெல்லும்
அனுபவத்தைக் குறைத்து விடும்.

பிறருடைய ஆற்றலை எடுத்துக் கொண்டால் என்ன ஆகும்?

ஆற்றல் என்பது பிறருடன் பகிர்ந்து
கொள்வதே. நம் திருப்திக்காக அல்ல.

நாம் கற்றுக் கொள்வதில் விடா முயற்சியாய் இருந்தால்?

உற்சாகத்தை உட்கொள்கிறோம்.

நாம் சுவாசித்து, நம்பி விடும் போது நாம்...?

நிச்சயம் உனக்குள்ளே எட்டிப்பார்!

ஒவ்வொரு சூழ்நிலையும் எப்படி இருக்க வேண்டும்?

நீ நினைப்பது போல் இல்லை.

கவனிப்பு என்பது?

சரியானவர்களுக்கு சரியான நேரத்தில் கொடுப்பது.

பட்டாம்பூச்சி தங்களுக்கு எதை நினைவு படுத்தும்?

குறுகிய காலத்தில் நிரந்தரமான வாழ்க்கை.

மேற்கோள்:

நிகழ்காலத்திலேயே வாழ்!

இனப்பெருக்கத்தைத் தவிர ஆண், பெண் எதற்கு படைக்கப் பட்டிருக்கிறார்கள்?

தீவிர பேரார்வத்துடன் பிணைப்பை வெளிப்படுத்த!

மொழிகளில் இந்தியா எவ்வாறு தனித்துவமாக விளங்குகிறது?

ஆழ்ந்த புதையலாய்!

நாட்காட்டியின் சம்பந்தம்?

இல்லை. நான் ஒருபோதும் கருத்தில் கொள்ள மாட்டேன். ஒவ்வொரு நாளும் ஒளி மயமே!

ஜல்லிக்கட்டு எதற்கு?

மனித சக்தியைக் காண்பிக்க. ரோமில் கூட இவ்விளையாட்டு உள்ளது.

மின்சார ஸ்விட்ச் எதற்கு?

மின்சாரத்தின் முனையை ஒழுங்குபடுத்த.

காய்கறிகள் உங்களுக்கு எவ்விதத்தில் ஈர்க்கின்றன? நறுக்கவா அல்லது சமைக்கவா?

வடிவங்கள் ஈர்க்கின்றன.

மின்சார ஸ்விட்ச் குறித்து?

நான் எலெக்ட்ரீசியன் இல்லை.

மேற்கோள்:

விநோதமான அகண்ட எண்ணங்களே எப்போதும் எல்லை!

அமைதி எவ்வாறு உதவும்?

பல நாள் எண்ணிக் கிடந்த விஷயங்களை ஒழுங்கு படுத்த.

விடுபடுதலின் பயம் என்றால் என்ன?

இறப்பின் வலி!

இன்றைய இளைஞர்களிடம் தனிமை உணர்வு பொதுவாக காணப்படுகிறது. அதன் காரணம்?

பொய்யான நிலைப்பாடு உருவாக்கப்படுகிறது.

உருவாக்குதல் என்பது என்ன?

பிழையில் பிறப்பது!

மனிதப் பிறப்பின் முக்கியத்துவம் என்ன?

தன்னைத் தூய்மைப் படுத்திக் கொள்ள!

யோகா என்பது என்ன?

குணப்படுத்தும் சிகிச்சை!

உள்ளிணைப்பு (inclusion) என்பது தங்களுக்கு?

மாறுபட்ட பார்வை!

பள்ளிக் கல்விமுறை குழந்தைகளிடம் எவ்வாறு மகிழ்ச்சியைக் கொண்டு வருகிறது?

எல்லா நிலையையும் எதிர் கொள்ளும் போது!

நேற்று நடந்த பஜனை குறித்து?

அமைதியில் திளைக்கும் சாய் பாபாவுக்கு சத்தம் நிறைந்த ஓதுதலாக இருந்தது.

ஹார்மோனியம் இசைக்கருவியும் அது தரும் உணர்வு குறித்து?

எல்லோரையும் விட அரவிந்த் நன்றாக வாசித்தான்.

மூளை ஒருபோதும் நெரிசலில் சிக்கிக் கொள்ளாது.

உங்களது கேள்வி?

தெற்கு சூடான் எங்குள்ளது?

**உங்களது சாப்பாட்டை முடிவு
செய்வதை எப்படி உணர்வீர்கள்?**

எனக்குள்ளே சந்தோஷ நிறைவு ஏற்படும்.

மரியாதை என்பது?

அடிப்படையாக ஒவ்வொரு மனிதனும்
கொண்டிருக்க வேண்டிய ஒன்று.

**கை ஒரு மனிதனுக்கு எதனை நினைவு
படுத்துகிறது?**

பூமியின் வேர்களை உணர!

அரவிந்தனின் காதுகள் எதற்கு?

கிசுகிசுவைக் கேட்க

யானை போல்!

ஏன் மூஞ்சுரு கணேசருக்கு வாகனமானது?

கணேசரைக் கேள்.

குடியரசு என்பது?

இந்திய வம்சாவளியை பிரகடனப்படுத்த

எப்படி நம் பண அமைப்பைக் கட்டமைத்தோம் என்று விவரிக்க!

கடவுளை எப்படி தினமும் அனுபவிக்க முடியும்?

மூச்சுக் காற்றின் மூலம்!

அடக்கம் எந்த அளவுக்கு முக்கியம்? அது எப்படி உதவும்?

மிக முக்கியம். ஒருவரின் வீரியம் அது.

தங்களுக்கு யானை எதனை நினைவுறுத்தும்?

மிகப்பெரிய வீரத்தை!

கடவுளின் பண்புகளை நாம் கொண்டிருக்க வேண்டுமா?

முற்றிலும் உண்மை!

சிறப்புக் குழந்தைகள் நலனில் மாநில அரசுக்கு தங்களது அறிவுரை என்ன?

வறுமைக் கோட்டுக்குக் கீழிருக்கும் குழந்தைகளைக் கல்வி சென்றடைய வேண்டும். அது அவர்களைத் திறனாளி ஆக்கும்.

மகிழ்ச்சியை எப்படி உள்வாங்கிக் கொள்வீர்கள்?

மன நிலை மகிழ்ச்சியில் உள்ளது.

குருகுலத்தில் இருக்கும் சிறப்புக் குழந்தைகளைத் தன்னிறைவு அடையச் செய்யும் எந்த மாதிரியான கல்வியைப் பரிந்துரைக்கிறீர்கள்?

வேலை வாய்ப்புக்கான தொழிற்கல்வியில் கவனம் செலுத்த வேண்டும்.

மாம்பழம் ஏன் பழங்களின் அரசன் எனப்படுகிறது?

அதன் ருசி அதிகம்.

விளையாட்டிலிருந்து என்ன நல்லொழுக்கம் கற்றுக் கொள்ள வேண்டும்?

ஆர்வம்

சுய ஒழுக்கம்

குழுவோடு பணிபுரிதல்

பிறரை ஊக்குவித்தல்

பூமியைப் பார்க்கும் போது அது என்ன நினைவூட்டுகிறது?

அமைதியான ஆனந்தம்

மனிதன் இக்கோளை மாசாக்குகிறான்.

ஆசிரியரைப் பற்றி

N. அரவிந்த் குமார் செப்டெம்பர் 5,1996ல் புதுடில்லியில் பிறந்தான். முதலில் நார்மலாகத்தான் இருந்தான். மூன்று வயதிலிருந்து ஆட்டிச நிலைக்கான அறிகுறிகள் தெரிய ஆரம்பித்தன.

அச்சிறு வயதிலேயே அவனது பிரச்சினைகளுடன் அரவிந்த் நிறைய சவால்களை சந்திக்க வேண்டியிருந்தது.

தன் 7ஆவது வயதில் அண்ணனை இழந்தான்.
தன் 14ஆவது வயதில் தனக்குத்
துணையாகவும் ரசிகனாகவும் இருக்கும்
தந்தையை இழந்தான்.

இதனால் சென்னைக்கு வர வேண்டிய
கட்டாயம் ஏற்பட்டது.

அரவிந்த்துக்கு நிறைய கேட்பது மிகவும்
பிடிக்கும். குறிப்பாக ஆங்கிலத்தின்
வார்த்தைகளை அவன் புரிந்து கொள்ளும்
விதமே அலாதி.

அவனது ஐந்தாவது வயதில் கம்ப்யூட்டரை
அறிமுகப் படுத்தினோம். அது அவனது
கருத்துப் புலமைக்கு (கம்யூனிகேஷனுக்கு),
தன் விருப்பு, வெறுப்புகளைத் தெரிவிப்பதற்கு
மற்றும் கற்றுக் கொள்வதற்கு புதிய
பாதையைத் திறந்து விட்டது.

அது மட்டுமின்றி, அவனது கம்யூனிகேஷன்
மூலம் அவனது ஆட்டிஸ நிலையில் அவன்
எதிர் கொள்ளும் சவால்களைப் பகிர்ந்து
கொள்ளும் போது அவனைப் பற்றிய புரிதலும்
அதிகரித்தது.

மனிதர்களின் இயல்பு, நகைச்சுவை உணர்வு,
கற்றுக் கொள்வதில் அவனது தீராத ஆர்வம்,

எல்லைகளைத் தகர்த்தல் ஆகியவை அவனது எழுத்தில் வெளி வந்தன.

திறந்த நிலைப் பள்ளி மூலம் 12ஆம் வகுப்பு முடித்தான். பின் ஹோட்டல் மேனேஜ்மெண்ட் மற்றும் போட்டோஷாப் டிப்ளமோவும் முடித்தான்.

எழுத்தாளராகவும் கவுன்சிலராகவும் (ஆற்றுப்படுத்துபவராக) இருந்து இவ்வுலகுக்கு குணமளிப்பதே அவனது ஆசை!